Extraordinary vegan

A L A ... TI ... E R

Book Publishing Company

SUMMERTOWN, TENNESSEE

Library of Congress Cataloging-in-Publication Data

Roettinger, Alan, 1952-
   Extraordinary vegan / Alan Roettinger.
      pages cm
   Includes index.
   ISBN 978-1-57067-296-5 (pbk.) — ISBN 978-1-57067-898-1 (e-book)
  1. Vegan cooking.   I. Title.
   TX837.R739 2013
   641.5'636—dc23

                   2013026301

Pictured on the cover: Quinoa with Zucchini, Basil, and Tomatoes, page 8
Pictured on the front flap: Quick Spicy Slaw (serving suggestion), page 79
Pictured on the back cover: Pears in Pomegranate Juice, page 134
Pictured on the back flap: Absinthe Ice Cream, page 128; Fresh Fig Tart in
   a Pistachio Crust, page 140

Calculations for the nutritional analyses in this book are based on the average
number of servings listed with the recipes and the average amount of an ingredient if a range is called for. Calculations are rounded up to the nearest gram.
If two options for an ingredient are listed, the first one is used. Not included
are optional ingredients and serving suggestions.

Photography: Andrew Schmidt
Food styling: Alan Roettinger
Cover and interior design: John Wincek

Book Publishing Company
PO Box 99
Summertown, TN 38483
888-260-8458
bookpubco.com

ISBN 13: 978-1-57067-296-5

Printed in Canada

19 18 17 16 15 14 13   9 8 7 6 5 4 3 2 1

Book Publishing Company is a member of
Green Press Initiative. We chose to print this
title on paper with 100% postconsumer
recycled content, processed without chlorine,
which saves the following natural resources:

- 73 trees
- 2,299 pounds of solid waste
- 34.340 gallons of water
- 6,331 pounds of greenhouse gases
- 33 million BTU of energy

For more information on Green Press Initiative,
visit greenpressinitiative.org.

Environmental impact estimates were made
using the Environmental Defense Fund
Paper Calculator. For more information, visit
papercalculator.org.

Printed on recycled paper

contents

foreword

In our research center in Washington, DC, we are continually surprised at the power of foods for health. A woman named Nancy joined one of our studies to see if she could lose weight and improve her diabetes. We guided her through some diet changes, and yes, she did lose a great deal of weight and her diabetes improved dramatically. But that was not all. One day, she realized that the arthritis pain that had bothered her for years had vanished too. Suddenly, she could open vacuum-packed jars with ease, she no longer winced when shaking hands, and she was able to throw her pain medicines away. A single change in eating habits had accomplished all these things in short order.

In another study, a man enrolled hoping to see if a menu change could help his chronic pain. And it did. But not only did healthy foods deliver on that promise, they also cured his erectile dysfunction!

A young woman came to our research center with terrible menstrual pains. She began a healthy diet, which not only eased her pain but also cured a hormone imbalance, leading to a sudden and surprising end to her long-standing infertility, much to her and her husband's surprise and delight.

This isn't magic. It's simple biology. When people shift to a menu drawn from healthful plant foods, animal fat and cholesterol are not in the diet anymore. And that allows the arteries to reopen, carrying blood and oxygen to all parts of the body. The body's basic biochemistry changes too, so that the insulin resistance that is the central problem in type 2 diabetes begins to retreat and the inflammation of rheumatoid arthritis melts away. Hormones that have long been askew come back into a more normal balance. People start to feel like themselves again.

When I was in medical school, we didn't envision any of this. I was taught that diabetes, arthritis, and artery blockages were a one-way street. But surprisingly enough, all of these problems can get dramatically better. Foods give you more power than you might have imagined

Taking advantage of that power isn't necessarily automatic, however. We need help in changing the way we eat. No matter how healthy foods may be, they have to work in our day-to-day lives. Recipes have to be reasonably quick and easy, and they have to be tasty. They need to be able to seduce us away from what we're eating now.

That's where *Extraordinary Vegan* comes in. Alan Roettinger knows how powerful foods can be. He takes no shortcuts in delivering recipes that are extraordinarily healthful, creative, and delicious. Each one is packed with the power of good nutrition.

Extraordinary Vegan is also an immensely practical book. It gives you the tricks you need and helps you to use them smartly. You will see when to add a special ingredient to crown a new dish and when to keep things simple and familiar. Once you've made a few of these recipes, you'll discover that you have acquired the art of knowing how to excite the senses and make eating a joy.

Let me encourage you then to dig into the other treasures in this book. Each one will teach you something new. See how far you can go. You'll be harnessing the power of healthful eating, and you'll feel the transformation physically and mentally. In the process, you'll be delighted at how great a healthy meal can taste, how great you feel, and how radiant you look.

Neal D. Barnard, MD

PRESIDENT, PHYSICIANS COMMITTEE FOR RESPONSIBLE MEDICINE
WASHINGTON, DC

My goal is to encourage and empower
as many people as possible
to make extraordinary food.
I want everyone to feel confident
and inspired to cook and eat at home.

ALAN ROETTINGER

acknowledgments

Above all and with great reverence, I would like to acknowledge the almighty breath, that humblest of breezes whose discreet coming and going is solely responsible for my existence. Yes, I said "whose," and it's no mistake, because that breath is life itself, and life is my dearest, most loyal friend. When I am sad, lonely, or agitated, and I remember to welcome that breath as it comes, everything slows down. Suddenly I'm not alone but at peace and full of joy. I could never adequately describe the gratitude I feel for the companionship of this beautiful friend, but I do want to acknowledge him. Her. It.

As a close second, I want to acknowledge the first person who gave me a shot as a private chef. He is a man who truly understands what perfection is and why it's so important to reach for it. Trying to hit that spot, to gratify his discerning palate, is what launched my entire career. For this, and for the kindness and respect he's always shown me, I owe a debt I can never repay.

As always, I must acknowledge my beautiful wife, whose support literally made this book possible. If you believe in divine blessings, then you might have an inkling of what a sublime gift she has been to me; if you don't, then good luck explaining how I ended up with her in my life. And my son, who has the unique ability to simultaneously be among my most incisive critics and most unwavering supporters. Earning their loyalty and faith in me is an invigorating project.

Finally, I would be remiss if I failed to acknowledge my publisher for believing in me enough to invest in a third adventure. My gratitude goes out to all the people at Book Publishing Company, whose collective talents have made this book possible, and to my editor, who continues to teach me how to write in my own first language. Just when I think I've got it, she finds a way to show me a better way to get my message across. Heartfelt thanks to all of them.

introduction

Over the course of more than thirty years as a private chef to the rich and famous, I've learned a few things about human nature. One insight in particular has served me well, both in my personal life and in my work: we are fundamentally creatures of hunger. This is good news to anyone who earns a living as a cook, but there is a great deal more to it than the obvious. We hunger for more than food. It's not enough that we satisfy our body's need to be replenished with nutrients; we need to enjoy the process. Enjoyment, in fact, is what we hunger for the most. It would be accurate to say that to enjoy—to feel joy—is our primary directive, driving every single one of our motives and activities.

This is why my clients hire me instead of asking their housekeeper to cook for them, as many other people do. They want more than basic sustenance. They want what everyone wants: surprise. It's been said that variety is the spice of life, but that's not exactly right. *Surprise* is the spice of life, and the only certain cure for boredom. Variety is wonderful, and thankfully the world is bursting with it. But what pleasure would it offer if it never surprised us, stopped us in our tracks, stunned us with unexpected beauty? The same moon rises every evening, yet every so often it catches us by surprise, perhaps appearing larger, fuller, brighter, or with an unusual hue, and we are spellbound by it.

Cooking is a profoundly enjoyable experience for me. I love the process, the sights and sounds, the colors, the aromas, the sheer alchemy of it all. But what inspires me most when I cook is the possibility of turning ordinary ingredients into an extraordinary eating experience. Some ingredients, like truffles or saffron, are exotic, and even in a minute quantity they infuse an entire dish with their ethereal presence. Others, like potatoes, are commonplace by themselves but become delectable when combined with a just few other ordinary ingredients, such as olive oil, rosemary, and garlic. And then there is a sovereign, irreplaceable ingredient that makes or breaks it for any cook. It cannot be measured, bought, borrowed, or, least of all, stolen. And guess what? I'm about to reveal it to you, dear reader, because I want you to succeed.

You've heard the expression "food made with love," right? Well, I was thinking about this and wondering what it might really mean. What difference would love make? If there was love in the food, how on earth would it have gotten there? Then I had an epiphany: *Attention is the currency of love.*

When I fell in love with my wife, I couldn't take my eyes off of her. I would listen intently to what she had to say, like it was the most interesting thing in the world. When I was at work or out running errands, I thought about her almost constantly. I might see something she'd like in a store, so I would buy it for her, excited by the thought of surprising her with it. Driving in my car, a song on the radio would remind me of her. My attention was literally flowing to her, even when she wasn't around. This is how love is conveyed. Giving our attention to other people—looking, listening, touching, pleasuring, caring—is the way love is transferred. People can feel it, and that's how they know we love them.

So how do you get love into food? By paying close attention to the way you prepare it. Pick the freshest, most eye-appealing ingredients. Wash and dry them well. Cut them cleanly and precisely into attractive shapes. Be careful to cook them in ways that preserve their inherent flavors and healthful properties. Think of innovative ways to showcase their unique attributes. Imagine them in combinations with other ingredients that will delight someone, especially someone with particular tastes. Lose yourself in the pleasure of the sights, sounds, and smells of the process. Present the food artfully, so it pleases the eye. Be in awe of your own creation. All of this focused attention infuses your food with love, and there will be something undeniably delightful about the experience of eating it.

All of the great chefs do this, and that's why people will travel long distances and pay high premiums to eat their food. Their long, arduous training makes them very disciplined and demanding about getting every detail just right, and their food is exquisite as a result.

Now, the chances of a home cook reaching the skill level of great chefs who hone their craft for decades are remote at best, but the fundamental rules of making extraordinary food are the same for everyone, and anyone can follow them to excellent results. That means you. Some rules are physical—like what happens to different ingredients when heat is applied, and how long each will take to reach an ideal state of texture and toothsomeness. These rules are best learned by experience, and if you follow my recipes, you'll pick them up intuitively over time. There are also a few rules that transcend the physical, the most important of which I'll share with you now.

Don't be intimidated. Making something good to eat is probably the most universal, oft-repeated activity in the world. As with any art, you *will* get good at it if you practice. Fortune favors the bold, so when you see an unfamiliar ingredient or what seems like an awfully long list of ingredients in a recipe, or if the recipe looks complicated to you, be fearless. Go for it without hesitation and do your best. If you're cooking for a discriminating gourmet, don't let that scare you either. People have often said to me, "Oh, I'd be afraid to cook for you—you're a chef!" Little did they know that food made by someone else is among a chef's favorite things in the world.

Don't worry about anything; just charge ahead. Make some mistakes and learn the ropes. Here's a sobering and liberating thought I've reflected on many times: My most spectacular culinary triumphs and my most humiliating disasters all wound up in the same place.

Always aim for the extraordinary. Even if you're just making mashed potatoes or oatmeal, try to make it extraordinarily tasty, with amazing texture and mouthwatering aroma. Make each component of every dish truly memorable. This may sound overdramatic, but if you cook this way, three things will happen: (1) you will put your full attention into what you do, infusing the food with that all-important, transcendent ingredient I mentioned above, (2) your skill level will improve significantly in a very short period of time, and (3) you'll enjoy yourself immensely, which is the whole point of doing anything. As a bonus, your food *will* be extraordinary, simply because you cared enough to give it your full attention.

Think outside the book. I'm sure that as you look through the recipes, you'll come across a few ingredients that are hard to find where you live, or perhaps cost more than you feel comfortable spending, or impart a flavor you just don't like. It's my book but it's *your* food, so don't be afraid to replace ingredients with others that better suit your taste or even omit ones you don't like. With time and practice, you'll acquire a sense of what works for you and how to make these substitutions. Take some calculated risks. Color outside the lines. Enjoy yourself! Before you know it, you'll be creating some original dishes of your own, and then you'll be outside the book for real. While you're at it, write down what you did; you never know where that might lead.

Finally, never stop at ordinary—
it's really not that much further to *extraordinary!*

CHAPTER 1

extraordinary ingredients
FOR YOUR EVERYDAY KITCHEN

Chiles and Chile Powders

AJÍ AMARILLO. A native of Peru, ají amarillo (literally "yellow chile") is similar to Aleppo pepper in that it imparts more flavor than heat. This makes it desirable for building complex layers of flavor in sauces, stews, and soups. It has an orange color that turns yellow when cooked into a dish. I use it in dried, ground form.

AJÍ PANCA. Another relatively mild native of Peru, ají panca has a fruity, almost berrylike, slightly smoky flavor. I like to combine it with ají amarillo and other chiles to create a garden of interesting background notes in soups and stews.

ALEPPO PEPPER. For people who don't tolerate spicy food very well, all chiles tend to taste the same, because once the heat begins, their taste buds go somewhat numb. Aleppo pepper, a native of northern Syria, is ideal for them, because it has a relatively mild bite combined with a lively flavor, reminiscent of sun-dried tomatoes. I use it frequently in my cooking because it allows me to pack chile flavor into a dish without making it too spicy.

ANCHO CHILE POWDER. Ancho chile is a ripened (red) dried Mexican poblano pepper (the fresh, green form is the pepper used for chiles rellenos). The flavor is exotic and quite strong, enough to alter the character of a dish dramatically.

CHIMAYÓ CHILE. Another chile that offers a complex flavor with relatively minor heat, the Chimayó of northern New Mexico is available only in dried, ground form in other areas. It brightens up salad dressings, grilled vegetables, and pretty much anything it touches.

RED CHILE POWDER. Indian grocery stores carry a very hot and fragrant red chile powder, but cayenne is a passable substitute.

Dried Herbs and Spices

BAHARAT. Used in the cuisines of Iraq and the Gulf states of the Arabian peninsula, baharat is a bright, lively spice mixture. Although it can be found in specialty shops, Middle Eastern grocery stores, and online (see Online Shopping Sources, page 143), baharat is easy to make at home. Put ¼ cup black peppercorns, 2½ tablespoons cumin seeds, 2 tablespoons coriander seeds, 2 tablespoons cloves, and 1 teaspoon cardamom seeds in a blender or spice mill. Process until finely ground. Transfer to a small bowl and stir in 2 tablespoons freshly grated or ground nutmeg, 2 tablespoons paprika, and 1½ tablespoons ground cinnamon. This will yield about 1 cup of baharat. Stored in a sealed container at room temperature, baharat will keep indefinitely.

GARAM MASALA. In Indian cuisine, garam masala (roughly translated as "hot spice mixture") is a blend of pungent aromatics ground together and used to enliven dishes with a vibrant note. The exact mixture varies from home to home and can contain any combination of bay leaves, black or green cardamom, cinnamon, cloves, coriander seeds, cumin, black cumin, nutmeg, mace, black or white peppercorns, or star anise (did I leave anything out?). The "heat" implied by the name refers to the pungent qualities of the spice mixture, not the stinging heat of chiles. Look for commercially prepared garam masala at Indian grocery stores or specialty stores, or purchase it online.

RAS EL HANOUT. A Moroccan spice mixture, available at Mediterranean and Arabic markets and at specialty stores, ras el hanout has a character similar in some ways to curry powder, imparting a complex, very fragrant, uniquely North African flavor. Ras el hanout means "top of the shop" in Arabic, indicating the shopkeeper's signature blend. In Morocco, the specific mixture varies from shop to shop and may contain well over twenty ingredients, including some unexpected ones like cassia bark, lavender, orris root, rosebuds, or even hashish, depending on the shopkeeper's expertise and predilection. Outside Morocco, most ras el hanout is commercially produced in France (sans the hashish) and is fairly standardized. My favorite comes from The

Spice House in Chicago (see Online Shopping Sources, page 143) and includes whole saffron threads.

SAFFRON THREADS. The saying "a little goes a long way" truly applies to saffron. A mere pinch will hurl a whole potful of whatever you're cooking into exotic terrains. Once the province of kings (it was worth more than its weight in gold), saffron comes from a purple crocus that yields only three threads (stigmas) per flower. Saffron is now much more affordable, in part because it is cultivated in Spain as well as in Kashmir. (See Online Shopping Sources, page 143).

SEA SALT. I keep both coarse and fine Celtic salt on hand for the best flavor and mineral content. A lot of people think that salt is just something to bring out the flavor of food—and it will—but good salt is much more than that. Hand-harvested salt from the ocean contains minerals and has a delicious flavor of its own that it will impart to the food. My favorite is actually not harvested from the sea, but it is the oldest sea salt on earth: Himalayan pink salt, formed millions of years ago as the world's highest peaks were pushed up from the ocean floor. Cool, huh?

SPANISH SMOKED PAPRIKA. Once a rare and hard-to-find item, Spanish smoked paprika is now fairly easy to track down. Like saffron, a small quantity of smoked paprika can go a long way in turning an ordinary dish in an extraordinary direction.

Fats

EXTRA-VIRGIN COCONUT OIL. If you're going to fry something, extra-virgin coconut oil is the best vegan medium for it. It's a highly saturated fat and remains quite firm at room temperature (unless you live in someplace like Guyana or Borneo). It has a strong but pleasant coconut flavor, which limits its application to dishes that go well with it, such as Southeast Asian, South Indian, Polynesian, Central and South American, and sub-Saharan.

FLAX OIL. I highly recommend using Udo's Oil 3•6•9 Blend, which combines flax with other seed oils in a blend that provides both omega-3 and omega-6 fatty acids in ideal proportions. Keep refrigerated.

WALNUT OIL. I use organic walnut oil on occasion for its mild, nutty flavor, which blends beautifully with mild vinegars to make a dressing for tender lettuces. Never cook with it, as heat will turn its delicate flavor bitter and destroy its antioxidant content. Keep refrigerated.

Seeds, Flavorings, Sweeteners, and Such

BLACK SESAME SEEDS. Very rich in minerals, black sesame seeds also contain phytosterols, which help lower cholesterol. Plus, they're delicious and make a beautiful garnish.

CHIA SEEDS. Native to Mesoamerica, chia seeds are a miraculous superfood, high in essential fats, fiber, protein, and minerals. Their hydrophilic quality enables them to absorb ten times their weight in water, which is useful for thickening puddings and other desserts. This characteristic is also valuable to athletes, because chia seeds soaked in water will release both their fat and the water slowly, helping athletes stay fueled and hydrated over an extended period.

MACA POWDER. Native to the Andes, maca is a tuber, regarded as a superfood for its adaptogenic properties. It is reputed to increase stamina, boost libido, reduce fatigue, and help cope with stress. I add it to smoothies.

MELLOW WHITE MISO. There are several varieties of miso (and I recommend trying them all), but mellow white miso is the most versatile because it combines well with other ingredients, adding a lightly salty, agreeably fermented (some would say cheesy-tasting) flavor. Miso is rich in live probiotics, so store it in the refrigerator and avoid cooking it, adding it instead after the cooking is done, as in miso soup.

MIRIN. Also known as sweet sake, mirin provides the distinctive flavor in teriyaki sauce. It is a rice wine similar to sake but sweeter and with a lower alcohol content. It adds a uniquely Japanese touch to sauces and condiments.

PALM SUGAR. A delectable alternative to brown sugar, palm sugar is harvested from coconut palms in Southeast Asia. It is available granulated and as a paste. Indian gur, or jaggery, made from sugarcane, is an acceptable substitute.

SRIRACHA SAUCE. A Vietnamese sweet-and-spicy red chile sauce, sriracha is now a fairly ubiquitous table condiment in Asian restaurants. This is a very useful ingredient, even in Western-oriented dishes, for adding a stab of heat. Sugar has been used for a long time in Chinese cooking to coax the heat and flavor out of chiles, and sriracha sauce does an excellent job of that.

TOMATO PURÉE. I prefer Italian passata di pomodoro, a minimally processed tomato purée, now widely available in glass jars rather than in cans. The beauty of reclosable jars is that you can use just a tablespoon or so to add tomato flavor to a dish and easily store the remaining purée for the next use.

VANILLA EXTRACT. Don't waste money on the cheap, flavorless stuff! Look for Tahitian vanilla or, at the very least, Madagascar bourbon vanilla. The cost is higher but the flavor is well worth it.

VEGETABLE BOUILLON CUBES, UNSALTED. One excellent way to add a mega splash of flavor to a soup, a sauce, or any juicy dish is to drop in a cube or two of vegetable bouillon. I threw one into mashed potatoes once, with striking results. I use it for pumping up rice and quinoa also.

Extraordinary food can be made with ordinary ingredients. In fact most ingredients are quite ordinary when you're in the country of their origin. Because most of the ingredients I use are bursting with flavor, small amounts of them will go a long way. As cooks, we can also augment the flavor of certain ingredients by using special techniques that can transform basic foods and seasonings and take them from ordinary to extraordinary. Simple treatments like infusing, reducing, roasting, or preserving can have a potent effect on how an ingredient tastes. Then, when we use these transformed ingredients in cooking, we begin the process with a distinct advantage.

extraordinary fundamentals

This chapter provides a glimpse of a few of my favorite preparations to have on hand. Some are for everyday use and others are for specific applications, but all of them will help you turn good food into great food. Eventually, you'll develop your own list of must-have items that you rely on to make your food stand out as extraordinary.

Quinoa is a wonderful gift to vegans and vegetarians. It provides bountiful protein, calcium, iron, magnesium, and fiber in respectable quantities, with very little fat. This is a basic recipe you can use for sweet or savory applications, but if you know you're going to use it in a savory dish, you can add a vegetable bouillon cube for extra flavor.

BASIC quinoa

MAKES 2½ CUPS

1 cup quinoa

1½ cups water

Pinch sea salt

1 unsalted vegetable bouillon cube (optional)

Rinse the quinoa and put it in a small saucepan. Add the water, salt, and optional bouillon cube. Bring to a boil over high heat. Decrease the heat to low, cover, and cook for 15 minutes. Fluff the grains with a silicone spatula. Stored in a sealed container in the refrigerator, the quinoa will keep for 3 days.

Per ½ cup: 136 calories, 4 g protein, 2 g fat (0 g sat), 24 g carbohydrates, 18 mg sodium, 32 mg calcium, 3 g fiber

TIP▶ An ancient grain originally grown in the Andes mountains of Peru, quinoa is now grown organically in the United States and is widely available in natural food stores and some supermarkets. It's rich in protein, is highly digestible, and has a distinctive texture and flavor. There are countless varieties of quinoa and many different colors. You'll mostly find white, red, and black quinoa in stores. White is the most common. Red quinoa is a bit firmer in texture, with a richer taste and a dark rust color. Black quinoa has a much firmer outer shell than white or red quinoa, so it requires longer cooking.

VARIATION▶ **Quinoa with Zucchini, Basil, and Tomatoes** (pictured on cover). Put 2 tablespoons olive oil in a skillet over medium-high heat and add 1 small onion, diced. Stir until soft, about 3 minutes. Add 2 small zucchini, quartered lengthwise and thinly sliced. Continue stirring until the zucchini is just tender, another 4 to five minutes. Add ¼ teaspoon salt and freshly ground black pepper to taste, and stir another 2 minutes. Stir in 1 cup cooked quinoa and 2 tablespoons coarsely chopped fresh basil. Stir until warmed through. Serve with fresh tomato slices.

GARLIC oil

This versatile condiment is ideal to use as a seasoning for steamed vegetables and baked potatoes or to enrich dips, soups, and sauces. Once prepared, garlic oil should be kept refrigerated in a dark glass bottle (see tip). Never heat the oil or add it to very hot foods, as this will damage the fragile omega-3 fats.

4 cloves garlic, minced or pressed
1 cup flax oil

Stir the garlic into the oil. Pour into a dark glass bottle and seal. Store in the refrigerator and use within 4 days.

Per 1 tablespoon: 121 calories, 0 g protein, 14 g fat (2 g sat), 0 g carbohydrates, 0 mg sodium, 14 mg calcium, 0 g fiber

TIP▶ The oil will keep for about 2 weeks after the bottle is opened, but the garlic will lose its punch and acquire a less-than-agreeable flavor after 3 to 4 days.

POOR MAN'S
aged balsamic vinegar

MAKES 2½ CUPS

Every now and then I like to splurge and buy a bottle of properly aged balsamic vinegar. While you can't fully replicate the effects of slow aging and gradual decanting over many years, this delicious option vaguely approximates the real thing, and it's done using a common culinary technique known as reduction. I recommend buying a large bottle of commercial balsamic vinegar and reducing it by a little less than half.

4 cups balsamic vinegar

Put the vinegar in a 2-quart enamel, glass, or stainless steel saucepan and bring to a boil over medium-high heat. Decrease the heat to medium-low and simmer until the vinegar is reduced to 2½ cups, 15 to 20 minutes. Pour the vinegar into a glass container and let cool. Sealed tightly and stored at room temperature, the vinegar will keep indefinitely.

Per 2 tablespoons: 45 calories, 0 g protein, 0 g fat (0 g sat), 9 g carbohydrates, 12 mg sodium, 12 mg calcium, 0 g fiber

Watch a video of Alan making aged balsamic vinegar.

youtu.be/Kc8w0QwfOzE

This luxuriously rich salad dressing is suitable for everyday use and special occasions alike. If you happen to have a bottle of properly aged balsamic vinegar, by all means use it. If you don't have aged balsamic vinegar on hand and haven't yet taken the time to prepare a batch of Poor Man's Aged Balsamic Vinegar, this recipe should inspire you to do so, as it will give you the extraordinary results that regular pedestrian balsamic vinegars can't match.

EXTRAORDINARY
balsamic vinaigrette

MAKES 1¾ CUPS

½ cup aged balsamic vinegar or Poor Man's
    Aged Balsamic Vinegar (opposite page)

2 tablespoons Dijon mustard

2 tablespoons freshly squeezed lemon
    juice (optional)

½ teaspoon sea salt

½ teaspoon freshly ground black pepper

½ cup flax oil

½ cup extra-virgin olive oil

Put the vinegar, mustard, optional lemon juice, salt, and pepper in a medium bowl and whisk until well blended. Add the flax oil and olive oil in a thin stream, whisking constantly, until the dressing has emulsified. Stored in a sealed glass jar in the refrigerator, the dressing will keep for about 1 week.

Per 2 tablespoons: 153 calories, 0 g protein, 16 g fat (2 g sat), 1 g carbohydrates, 133 mg sodium, 0 mg calcium, 1 g fiber

See Alan preparing vinaigrette.
youtu.be/yoZq17wRARA

Some people don't sleep well if they eat raw garlic in the evening, but they have little or no trouble if the garlic is thoroughly cooked. Slow-roasting garlic tames its pungent, stimulating qualities considerably. Roasted garlic imparts a uniquely delicious flavor to food, so I like to keep a modest supply on hand for this purpose alone. Use the whole cloves or mash them into a purée to add to salad dressings, sauces, soups, beans, or sautéed vegetables.

ROASTED garlic

MAKES 2 CUPS

2 cups peeled garlic cloves, root ends trimmed

2 tablespoons extra-virgin olive oil

½ teaspoon sea salt

¼ teaspoon freshly ground black pepper

Watch Alan preparing roasted garlic.

youtu.be/XZ4rPoORWTo

Preheat the oven to 375 degrees F.

Put the garlic in a medium bowl. Add the oil, salt, and pepper and toss until evenly coated.

Stack 10 sheets of heavy-duty aluminum foil on a work surface, crumpling them slightly so they don't lie flat. This will create some air pockets, which will act as heat buffers to prevent the garlic from burning. Put a sheet of parchment paper on top of the stack of foil. Pile the garlic mixture into a mound in the center of the paper and fold the entire stack of paper and foil over it, folding and crimping the edges to form a tight seal.

Put the package directly on the oven rack and bake for 45 minutes. Decrease the oven temperature to 325 degrees F, and bake for 15 minutes longer. Remove the package from the oven and let cool completely.

Open the package and slide the garlic into a glass jar, along with the oil and any accumulated juices. Covered tightly and stored in the refrigerator, the garlic will keep for 3 weeks.

Per 2 tablespoons: 29 calories, 1 g protein, 2 g fat (0.2 g sat), 3 g carbohydrates, 70 mg sodium, 0 mg calcium, 1 g fiber

Hazelnuts, more than any nut I know, become transcendental when roasted and are quite addictive. Roasting loosens their bitter skins, enabling the cook to remove them entirely. Roasted hazelnuts add an assertive flavor boost to any dish or component they land in—salads, soups, sauces, pilafs, desserts— and they positively reign supreme in combination with chocolate.

ROASTED hazelnuts

MAKES 4 CUPS

4 cups hazelnuts

See Alan roasting and peeling hazelnuts.
youtu.be/PZdCSbRqzp8

Preheat the oven to 400 degrees F.

Spread the hazelnuts on a baking pan in a single layer. Roast for 7 to 10 minutes, until they are aromatic, the skins are blistered, and the flesh underneath is exposed and lightly browned. Check them often, as there is a fine line between a perfectly roasted hazelnut and one that has begun to burn. Immediately slide the hazelnuts onto a large kitchen towel. Gather them into the center of the towel and fold the sides over them to encase them snugly. Carefully turn the resulting package over, so the folded ends are underneath, securing them in place. Let the nuts steam in their own heat for about 10 minutes.

Without loosening the towel, knead the bundle firmly for 1 to 2 minutes, rubbing the nuts against one another inside the towel. This will remove most if not all of the skins. Carefully turn over and open the bundle. Lift a handful of the nuts at a time, opening your fingers slightly to sift out any skins that may cling. Put the clean nuts in a bowl. Repeat with the remaining nuts, and then discard the skins. Stored in a sealed container in the freezer, the nuts will keep indefinitely (unless you remember they're there and decide to eat just one...).

Per ¼ cup: 212 calories, 5 g protein, 20 g fat (2 g sat), 6 g carbohydrates, 0 mg sodium, 35 mg calcium, 2 g fiber

Go for Extraordinary! It's essential to use the freshest hazelnuts you can get your hands on. How do you know if they're fresh? The test is quite simple—just taste them. They should have a little snap to them when you bite down and a very agreeable flavor, with no hint of rancidity. If you like the taste, they're fresh enough for you.

The smell of peppers roasting is an unsurpassed aromatherapy treatment for kitchen, cook, and home. Roasted peppers can be eaten as they are, used in sandwiches or salads, or served alongside olives, marinated artichokes, and pickled onions as an appetizer. Make a lightning-quick spicy red

roasted PEPPERS

MAKES 1½ CUPS

6 organic bell peppers, red, green, yellow, orange, or a combination

Preheat the broiler. Line a baking sheet with aluminum foil.

Quarter the peppers lengthwise and remove the stems and membranes. Don't worry about any seeds that may adhere—they will actually add flavor. Trim the pointed tips so the peppers will lie flat, cut-side down. Put the peppers on the prepared baking sheet and broil until the skins are evenly charred, about 10 minutes. Immediately put the peppers in a small bowl and cover tightly with a pot lid, a plate, or aluminum foil. Repeat with the remaining peppers. Let the peppers steam in the bowl until they are barely warm, about 15 minutes. Uncover and pour cold water into the bowl to loosen the skins. Remove and discard the skins. Stored in a jar in the refrigerator, the peppers will keep for 1 week.

Per ¼ cup: 24 calories, 1 g protein, 0 g fat (0 g sat), 6 g carbohydrates, 4 mg sodium, 10 mg calcium, 2 g fiber

Watch Alan roast and peel peppers.

youtu.be/LZF9G6tNbdw

pepper sauce by whirling some roasted peppers in a blender with a little garlic, hot red chile powder, and salt. Mixed roasted peppers are the main ingredient in Peperonata (page 32), and roasted red peppers are a primary component of Romesco Sauce (page 30).

TIP▶ If you plan to use the peppers in a recipe (such as Peperonata) in which they will be cooked further, plunge them into a bowl of cold water as soon as you remove them from the broiler (rather than letting them steam in a covered bowl). The skins will be slightly more difficult to remove, but the peppers won't get mushy when cooked in other recipes.

TIP▶ I've gotten a lot of practice, so it takes only a few minutes for me to roast and peel my own red peppers, but for most people it will save a lot of trouble to just buy a jar or two and keep them on hand. (Even I do this when time is extremely tight.) Just be sure to rinse them well before using to get rid of the taste of the bottled liquid, and also remove the seeds and any burned skin that may still be clinging to them.

Go for Extraordinary! To store the roasted peppers longer or simply to suffuse them with extra flavor, toss them in a bowl with ¼ cup of extra-virgin olive oil, 2 cloves of garlic thinly sliced, ¼ teaspoon of sea salt, and a pinch of freshly ground black pepper. Pack the mixture into a glass jar. Sealed tightly and stored in the refrigerator, the peppers will keep for 3 weeks.

PRESERVED lemons

Among the everyday components of Moroccan food that make it starkly unique are preserved lemons. They can be found in specialty shops and Middle Eastern markets, packed in small jars. But for a fraction of the cost, they can be easily made at home, as they are in homes all over Morocco. Their flavor is unparalleled—an amazing blend of sweet, sour, salty, and bitter. Even one-quarter of a preserved lemon, sliced or diced and added to a salad or stew, can alter the character of the dish dramatically. The brine itself can be used instead of salt to impart flavor to salad dressings, sauces, and soups.

10 unblemished organic lemons, preferably Meyer lemons, washed well
10 tablespoons coarse sea salt, preferably Celtic salt
Freshly squeezed lemon juice, as needed

Cut into the lemons as if to quarter them lengthwise, leaving the last ¾ inch of them intact at the stem end. Spread a lemon open and pack about 1 tablespoon of the salt into the cuts. Repeat with the remaining lemons, using 1 tablespoon of salt for each one. Put the salted lemons in a sterilized 1-quart jar (see note), pressing down on them with a wooden spoon to squeeze the juice out and pack them in firmly. Be careful not to tear the skin. The goal is to squeeze out enough juice to cover all the lemons, but this may not occur right away. Press down as much as possible without tearing the lemons. Seal the jar and put it in a cool, dark place for 8 to 12 hours.

Open the jar and again press down on the lemons with a wooden spoon to encourage more juice to seep out. This time, more juice will be expressed and should cover (or mostly cover) the lemons. Seal the jar and again put it in a cool, dark place for 8 to 12 hours.

Learn how to make preserved lemons.
youtu.be/VmRIGqeVBlk

Press down on the lemons again to extract more juice and compact them. If the lemon juice doesn't cover the lemons, add additional freshly squeezed lemon juice as needed until they are fully submerged. Seal the jar and return it to a cool, dark place. Let the lemons macerate for 1 month.

After 1 month the lemons will be preserved, and you can begin using them. They will have become quite soft, with a silky smooth texture. Stored in a sealed jar in the refrigerator, the lemons will keep indefinitely.

Per ½ lemon: 10 calories, 0 g protein, 0 g fat (0 g sat), 3 g carbohydrates, 0 mg sodium, 5 mg calcium, 1 g fiber

TIP▶ To sterilize the jar, wash and rinse it thoroughly, and then fill it with boiling water. After 1 minute, empty the jar and let it air-dry.

VARIATION▶ Replace the lemons with 12 limes and the lemon juice with freshly squeezed lime juice.

KOMBU dashi

Kombu dashi is a very simple seaweed broth used in a number of Japanese soups, sauces, and salad dressings. In traditional Japanese cuisine, this broth is made with kombu (a flat, dark-green seaweed) and shaved dried bonito fish. I find the flavor is not significantly different when the shaved fish is omitted, and this works out very well for the fish.

1 (4-inch) **piece kombu**
4¼ cups cold water

Rinse the kombu very quickly under running water and break into several small pieces. Put the pieces in a small pot and cover with the water. Heat over very low heat; do not allow the water to come to a boil. Let the water hover just below a simmer for about 10 minutes. Remove from the heat and let cool. Remove the kombu. Stored in a glass container in the refrigerator, dashi will keep for 1 week.

Per 1 cup: 0 calories, 0 g protein, 0 g fat (0 g sat), 0 g carbohydrates, 15 mg sodium, 0 mg calcium, 0 g fiber

NOTE▶ The leftover kombu can be cut and used in seaweed salads, soups, and other dishes.

This recipe is a staple that you can use for many applications, depending on what other ingredients you add to it. Sweetened cashew cream is used in making dairy-free desserts, and unsweetened cashew cream can enrich savory items, such as soups and sauces. Bear in mind that cashew cream is highly perishable, so when you make a batch, be prepared to use it all within two to three days.

cashew CREAM

MAKES 2 CUPS

2 cups raw cashews, preferably whole

¼ cup water, plus more as needed

Put the cashews in a medium bowl and cover with water by at least 2 inches. Let soak for 8 to 12 hours at room temperature (see tip).

Drain and rinse the cashews and put them in a blender. Add the water and process until smooth. If it is difficult to process the cashews, add a little more water, 1 tablespoon at a time, as needed. Bear in mind that you may want to add other liquids to the cream later, so the less water you add during processing, the better, as otherwise the cream may become too thin. Stored in a sealed container in the refrigerator, cashew cream will keep for 2 to 3 days.

Per ¼ cup: 150 calories, 5 g protein, 12 g fat (2 g sat), 8 g carbohydrates, 0 mg sodium, 20 mg calcium, 1 g fiber

TIP▶ If you're in a hurry, you can speed up the soaking process. Pour boiling water over the cashews and let them soak for 1 hour. The first method is preferable because nuts contain fragile fats that don't tolerate heat very well, but the second will work in a pinch.

Go for Extraordinary! Whole cashews will yield a whiter, superior cream compared to broken cashew pieces.

SWEET CASHEW CREAM▶ Add ¼ cup of maple syrup to the blender before processing. If appropriate for the application, you can also add 1 teaspoon vanilla, almond, or other extract and 3 tablespoons liqueur, such as kirsch or amaretto.

Watch Alan make cashew cream.

youtu.be/W1blFimQv1g

Chocolate ganache is used in truffles, cake fillings, and pastries. The standard ratio used in French pastry making is typically equal amounts of chocolate and cream, but I've created an extraordinary nondairy version. Anyone who has experience working with chocolate may blanch at the thought of adding water to melted chocolate (it's common knowledge that water ruins chocolate), but trust me, this works. I add flax oil at the end to contribute richness to the ganache, which would normally come from the fat in the cream. The flax oil also adds a healthful quality to the mixture, providing omega-3 fatty acids.

CHOCOLATE ganache

MAKES 2 CUPS

8 ounces dark chocolate, chopped

¾ cup hot water

¼ cup flax oil

2 tablespoons liqueur (optional)

Put the chocolate in a double boiler or a bowl set over hot but not boiling water. Stir until melted. Add 2 tablespoons of the hot water to the chocolate and whisk gently to incorporate. Add another 2 tablespoons of the hot water and stir. The mixture will appear to break and seize up at first, but continue stirring and adding the hot water, 2 tablespoons at a time, until it begins to flow again. When all the water has been added, stir in the oil, followed by the optional liqueur. Let cool completely. Cover and refrigerate until firm, about 2 hours.

Per 2 tablespoons: 62 calories, 1 g protein, 5 g fat (2 g sat), 3 g carbohydrates, 0 mg sodium, 4 mg calcium, 1 g fiber

Go for Extraordinary! The hot water can be infused with various spices, herbs, teas, or extracts prior to using, depending on the final application. The liqueur will also depend on your planned use of the ganache.

See Alan making chocolate ganache and offering serving suggestions.

youtu.be/ezvEJbY38h4

The first thing you eat in the morning has the potential to set you up for the rest of the day, for better or worse. It can influence the way you feel, how effectively you work, and whether or not you make wise choices about what you eat later in the day. Just like "getting up on the wrong side of the bed" can set you on a ruinous, punishing trajectory, making poor food choices in the morning can start you off on the wrong foot diet-wise, setting you up to eat harmful junk you later regret.

Conversely, by eating fresh, nutrient-dense food at your morning meal, you're in effect taking control of your choices from the outset, and empowering your body to be in charge of its needs. It will be much easier to listen to the messages your body sends to you if you begin the day by giving it clean fuel.

breakfast

Not every day calls for the same kind of breakfast. For example, if I'm going to be standing and cooking all day, a substantial breakfast, like a big bowl of oatmeal with dried fruits and nuts, is ideal. But if I'll be sitting at a desk writing for most of the day, that breakfast would put me right to sleep. So a light, protein-rich smoothie (see pages 46 and 47) would be a much better choice.

Choose your breakfast with awareness, and then pay attention to how you feel after you eat it. That way, you can adjust what you eat the remainder of the day accordingly. The body is a very effective communicator, but that only helps us if we listen and respond appropriately. Breakfast is a good place to start this partnership.

Tarahumaras and other natives of the American Southwest and northern Mexico have been known to routinely run one hundred miles without stopping, on just a handful of chia seeds, a bonafide superfood. I make a chia-based drink called *agua de chia*, or *chia fresca*, which has been popular in Mexico since pre-Columbian times. For more drinks using chia seeds, see pages 44 and 48.

TARAHUMARA running food

MAKES 1 SERVING

2 cups water

3 tablespoons chia seeds (see page 4)

Juice of ½ lime

½ teaspoon palm sugar (optional)

Put all the ingredients in a bowl or a large glass and stir briskly for at least 30 seconds. It's important to keep the seeds moving as they begin to absorb the water to prevent them from clumping. Let sit for 10 minutes, and then stir again. Serve at once.

Per serving: 185 calories, 9 g protein, 9 g fat (0 g sat), 17 g carbohydrates, 1 mg sodium, 243 mg calcium, 15 g fiber

VARIATION▶ For serious runners and athletes, add 1 tablespoon of liquid coenzyme Q10 (CoQ10) with L-carnitine, 2 teaspoons of D-ribose powder, and 1½ teaspoons of creatine monohydrate powder. These supplements combine to help boost energy production in muscle cells and prevent fatigue. L-carnitine is essential for fat burning.

Peperonata, page 32

Avocado Relish with Preserved Lemon, *page 36*

Pickled Red Onions in Blood Orange Juice, page 42

Raw Beet Wrap, page 56

miso broth WITH GINGER

On cold mornings, I enjoy the warmth of a simple miso broth and the benefits of the probiotics it contains. It's important not to boil miso, as heat will damage the beneficial enzymes, so be sure to follow the directions below to the letter.

2 tablespoons mellow white miso

1 teaspoon grated fresh ginger

1½ cups Kombu Dashi (page 18) **or water**

1 teaspoon reduced-sodium tamari (optional)

1 teaspoon mirin (optional)

Put the miso and ginger in a small bowl. Put the dashi in a small saucepan and bring to a simmer over medium-high heat. Remove from the heat and let sit for 20 seconds. Pour about ¼ cup of the dashi over the miso and stir until well combined. Add the remaining dashi and stir well. Stir in the optional tamari and mirin. Serve at once.

Per serving: 62 calories, 4 g protein, 2 g fat (0 g sat), 6 g carbohydrates, 1,580 mg sodium, 0 mg calcium, 2 g fiber

VARIATION▶ For a slightly more substantial version, add ½ cup of cooked brown rice to the broth. Cooked brown rice can be frozen in small portions for just this sort of last-minute occasion. Cooked brown rice can also be found in the frozen food aisle at natural food stores. Whether using frozen or leftover rice, warm it first so it won't cool the broth.

This is my summertime option to cooked oatmeal. Not only is it cool and refreshing, but it's also raw, which helps to preserve heat-sensitive nutrients. If you happen to be out of one or more of the ingredients, feel free to substitute with what you have on hand; for instance, any kind of berries can be used instead of blueberries. As long as you've got the oats and some kind of juice, the rest is entirely a matter of personal taste.

NUTRIENT-DENSE muesli

MAKES 4 SERVINGS

1½ cups old-fashioned rolled oats

1 cup unsweetened shredded dried coconut

1 cup sliced almonds

½ cup buckwheat groats

½ cup raw pumpkin seeds

½ cup raw sunflower seeds

½ cup hempseeds

½ cup dried currants

½ cup goji berries (optional)

2 tablespoons chia seeds

4½ cups apple juice or other juice

2 apples

1 cup frozen wild blueberries, thawed (optional)

Combine the oats, coconut, almonds, buckwheat, pumpkin seeds, sunflower seeds, hempseeds, currants, optional goji berries, and chia seeds in a large bowl. Add the juice and stir well. Cover and refrigerate for 8 to 12 hours. Just before serving, grate the apples into the bowl, add the optional blueberries, and stir until evenly distributed.

Per serving: 893 calories, 28 g protein, 46 g fat (3 g sat), 104 g carbohydrates, 93 mg sodium, 94 mg calcium, 17 g fiber

TIP▸ If you're eating alone or serving fewer than four people, the unused portion of muesli can be stored in the refrigerator and served the following day. Alternatively, you can mix the dry ingredients and add a portion of the juice to just the muesli you expect to use the following morning, saving the rest for another day. Stored in a sealed container in the refrigerator, the dry mixture will keep for 3 weeks.

NUTRIENT-DENSE oatmeal

MAKES 2 SERVINGS

Instead of combining the oats with water and salt first, and then bringing them to a boil, bring the water to a boil first, and then stir in the oats. The result will be more like cooked grain than a gooey gruel, especially when you use the proportion of water to oats in this recipe. Almonds, pumpkin seeds, and flax oil add all the richness of butter but with many more nutrients.

2 cups water

1 apple, cut into bite-sized pieces

1 peach, cut into bite-sized pieces
   (optional)

1 teaspoon vanilla extract

¼ cup goji berries (optional)

¼ cup dried currants

Pinch sea salt

1 cup old-fashioned rolled oats

½ cup raw almonds

½ cup pumpkin seeds

¼ cup flax oil

2 tablespoons maple syrup (optional)

Combine the water, apple, optional peach, vanilla extract, optional goji berries, currants, and salt in a medium saucepan and bring to a boil over medium-high heat. Add the oats all at once and stir well. Return to a boil, cover, and decrease the heat to low. Cook for 5 minutes. Remove from the heat, stir once, cover, and let sit for 30 to 60 seconds. Portion into two bowls and top with the almonds, pumpkin seeds, oil, and optional maple syrup. Serve at once.

Per serving: 814 calories, 22 g protein, 59 g fat (5 g sat), 60 g carbohydrates, 36 mg sodium, 84 mg calcium, 12 g fiber

CREAM OF quinoa

The texture of quinoa and the creaminess of coconut milk are a fabulous approximation of cooked cream of wheat. You may find it's more than sweet enough without any added sweetener, especially with the crushed cardamom.

1 cup Basic Quinoa (page 8)
1 cup full-fat coconut milk
4 green cardamom pods
1 banana, sliced (optional)

Put the quinoa and coconut milk in a small saucepan. Put the cardamom pods on a cutting board and crush them with a wooden spoon. Pry out the seeds and discard the pods. Crush the seeds into a coarse powder using the back of the wooden spoon and add to the quinoa. Cook over medium heat, stirring frequently, until the mixture begins to simmer, about 2 minutes. Add the optional banana, stir, and remove from the heat. Serve at once.

Per serving: 694 calories, 11 g protein, 46 g fat (36 g sat), 57 g carbohydrates, 96 mg sodium, 64 mg calcium, 6 g fiber

Like quinoa, buckwheat is a seed, not a grain, and it's also gluten-free. Because buckwheat isn't starchy like grain cereals, both kasha (toasted buckwheat) and untoasted buckwheat are easily digested and won't weigh you down the way grains often do. They're also rich in protein.

kasha
WITH SWEET RED PEPPER AND ZUCCHINI

MAKES 1 SERVING

4 cups water

¼ teaspoon salt

½ cup kasha

1 teaspoon extra-virgin olive oil

½ onion, diced

½ red bell pepper, diced

1 small zucchini, diced

¼ teaspoon smoked paprika

1 tablespoon Garlic Oil (page 9)

2 tablespoons chopped fresh parsley (optional)

Put the water in a medium saucepan with a pinch of the salt. Bring to a boil over high heat. Stir in the kasha and return to a boil. Decrease the heat to medium-low, cover, and cook until the kasha is tender but firm, about 12 minutes. Drain.

Put the olive oil in a skillet over medium-high heat. Add the onion and cook, stirring almost constantly, for about 1½ minutes. Add the red pepper and cook, stirring almost constantly, for 1½ minutes. Add the zucchini, paprika, and remaining salt and stir well. Decrease the heat to medium and cook, stirring frequently, until the vegetables are just tender, about 5 minutes. Add the kasha and heat, stirring frequently, until warmed through. Remove from the heat and stir in the garlic oil and optional parsley. Serve at once.

Per serving: 293 calories, 5 g protein, 19 g fat (3 g sat), 6 g carbohydrates, 582 mg sodium, 41 mg calcium, 6 g fiber

CHAPTER 4

sauces, dips, and condiments

Back in the early, pre-refrigeration days of classic French cooking, sauces came about specifically as a means of covering up the foul taste of decomposing meat and fish (charming!). What a difference a couple of centuries make. Sauces, and their cousins, dips and condiments, are now celebrated dishes in their own right, known and appreciated for their specific qualities and uses. I could write a lengthy cookbook on these three players alone.

A recent addition to my repertoire is romesco sauce. I happened to see small jars of a commercially prepared salsa romesco in a specialty store one day, and my curiosity got the best of me, so I brought a jar home. The sauce was interesting, but like so many commercial products, it was also disappointing. Still, I could tell that the original version of this sauce must have been quite special, so I set about tracking down a few recipes that might unlock the secret of a true romesco. I tinkered with them and came up with two versions I liked (loved!), and included the simpler, easier one in this chapter.

I mention this one sauce anecdote because I want to illustrate how easy it is to branch out, explore, and adopt new preparations and techniques. Sauces and condiments are especially versatile. One sauce can be used for several applications, as you'll see, and a slightly altered version of it can be used for even more. Also, it's often easy to adjust a nonvegan recipe to make it vegan.

A staple of the cuisine of Catalonia, in northeastern Spain, romesco sauce is a profoundly gratifying condiment. It is traditionally served with grilled foods, on which indeed it excels, and it goes very well with boiled or baked potatoes. It also makes a compelling dip, an assertive sandwich spread, and an irresistible thing to lick off one's fingers. The quantity may seem excessive, so feel free to cut it in half. However, I've learned that with exquisite dishes that require a little work, you might as well make a lot while you're at it. You won't be sorry, believe me.

romesco SAUCE

MAKES 5 CUPS

6 red bell peppers

2 cups Roasted Hazelnuts (page 13)

½ cup red wine vinegar

½ cup extra-virgin olive oil

½ cup flax oil

24 cloves Roasted Garlic (page 12)

3 tablespoons Spanish smoked hot paprika

3 tablespoons salt-free tomato paste

1 teaspoon hot red chile powder or cayenne

1 teaspoon salt

Preheat the broiler. Line a baking sheet with aluminum foil.

Quarter the peppers lengthwise and remove the stems and membranes. Don't worry about any seeds that may adhere—they will actually add flavor. Trim the pointed tips so they will lie flat, cut-side down. Put a single layer of the peppers on the prepared baking sheet skin-side up and broil for 10 to 15 minutes, until the skins are evenly blackened. Immediately put the peppers in a small bowl and cover tightly with a pot lid, a plate, or aluminum foil. Repeat with the remaining peppers. Let the peppers steam in the bowl until barely warm, about 15 minutes. Uncover and pour cold water into the bowl to loosen the skins. Remove and discard the skins.

Put the peppers in a blender. Add the hazelnuts, vinegar, olive oil, flax oil, garlic, paprika, tomato paste, chile powder, and salt. Process until smooth, stopping occasionally to scrape down the blender jar. Stored in sealed glass jars in the refrigerator, the sauce will keep for 2 weeks.

Per ¼ cup: 199 calories, 3g protein, 20 g fat (2 g sat), 6 g carbohydrates, 119 mg sodium, 8 mg calcium, 3 g fiber

Classic pesto Genovese is a longstanding love of mine, but I've had to forgo the pleasure ever since I stopped eating dairy products. For a guy like me, making pesto seemed a joyless prospect without the traditional cheeses that give it that rich, uniquely tangy flavor. Then one day my wife was making her own version of pesto and we had no pine nuts. I suggested macadamias for their vaguely similar texture. She had me taste the pesto before she added the cheese. Oof! What a flavor! I think even my Italian great-nonna would have gone for this.

VEGAN pesto

4 cups fresh basil leaves, packed

1 cup raw macadamia nuts or raw Brazil nuts

¼ cup extra-virgin olive oil, plus more as needed

2 cloves garlic, minced or pressed, plus more as needed

½ teaspoon sea salt, plus more as needed

Put the basil, nuts, oil, garlic, and salt in a food processor. Pulse until the basil and nuts are finely chopped, stopping occasionally to scrape down the work bowl. Taste and add more salt and garlic if desired. Scrape into a glass or stainless steel container and smooth out the top. Pour a small amount of olive oil on top and tip the container to coat the surface evenly. This will prevent discoloration.

Covered tightly, the pesto will keep for 1 week in the refrigerator or 3 months in the freezer. For the best flavor, bring to room temperature before using.

Per 2 tablespoons: 52 calories, 1 g protein, 6 g fat (1 g sat), 1 g carbohydrates, 41 mg sodium, 14 mg calcium, 1 g fiber

TIP▶ Pesto is traditionally used as a sauce for pasta, but it also makes a brilliant sandwich spread. It also does wonders for a baked potato or even boiled potatoes. Even unaccompanied and unembellished, right from a spoon, it's irresistible. Truly.

This classic Italian dish is like a drug to me, a sublime comfort food. It can be served as a vegetable dish, a condiment, or a sauce with pasta or polenta. It's a delicious breakfast or brunch item, served on toast or alongside potatoes. You may think this

peperonata

See photo facing page 22.

MAKES 10 CUPS

6 red bell peppers

3 orange bell peppers

3 yellow bell peppers

3 green bell peppers

¼ cup extra-virgin olive oil

3 large yellow onions

12 cloves garlic, thinly sliced

24 ounces no-salt-added tomato purée, preferably Italian *passata di pomodoro*

1 tablespoon red wine vinegar

2 teaspoons evaporated cane juice crystals

1 teaspoon salt

2 bay leaves

½ teaspoon hot red chile powder or cayenne, plus more as needed

Freshly ground black pepper

Preheat the broiler. Line a baking sheet with aluminum foil.

Quarter the peppers lengthwise and remove the stems and membranes. Trim the pointed tips so they will lie flat, cut-side down. Put a single layer of the peppers on the prepared baking sheet, skin-side up, and broil for 10 to 15 minutes, until the skins are evenly blackened. Immediately drop the roasted peppers into a large bowl of cold water. Repeat with the remaining peppers. If the water becomes warm during the process, drain it from the bowl and add fresh cold water. When all the peppers have been broiled and cooled, remove and discard the skins, along with any seeds. Cut the peppers into 1½-inch squares and put them in a clean bowl.

Put the olive oil in a large soup pot over high heat until fragrant, about 30 seconds. Add the onions and stir well. Cook, stirring occasionally, until the onions are soft and lightly browned at the edges, 2 to 5 minutes. Add the garlic and cook, stirring

makes an awful lot—and if you do, feel free to cut this recipe in half—but you'll be surprised how fast it disappears, and how sorry you'll be to see the last of it go. Slurp, slurp—*like a drug, I tell you!*

constantly, for 2 minutes. Add the peppers, along with any accumulated juices in the bowl, and stir well. Cook, stirring frequently, until the mixture is nearly dry, 10 to 15 minutes. Add the tomato purée, vinegar, evaporated cane juice crystals, salt, bay leaf, and chile powder. Stir until the mixture is boiling, and then decrease the heat to low. Taste and add more chile powder if desired. Cover and cook until the vegetables are very tender and the juices have reduced to a thick sauce, 1 to 1½ hours. Season with black pepper to taste.

Stored in sealed glass jars in the refrigerator, the peperonata will keep for 2 weeks. If no one is home, that is.

Per ½ cup: 62 calories, 2 g protein, 3 g fat (0.4 g sat), 9 g carbohydrates, 123 mg sodium, 48 mg calcium, 3 g fiber

Go for Extraordinary! For a slight twist that ramps up the extraordinary factor even higher, add just a pinch of saffron stamens during the last 20 minutes of cooking—and I really mean just a pinch! Any more than that will overwhelm the flavor of the peppers.

Guacamole has been a favorite in Mexico since long before the Spanish invasion. The name comes from a contraction of two words in *nahautl*, the language of the Aztecs: *ahuacatl* (avocado) and *mulli* (sauce). This version includes four

TOMATILLO guacamole

MAKES 3 CUPS

3 large or 4 medium tomatillos

2 poblano chiles

3 ripe avocados

¼ cup freshly squeezed lime juice

1 tablespoon extra-virgin olive oil

½ teaspoon salt, plus more as needed

1 small white onion, finely diced

2 serrano chiles, finely diced, plus
   more as needed

1 cup coarsely chopped fresh
   cilantro leaves and tender stems,
   lightly packed

Remove the dry, papery skin from the tomatillos and wash off the slimy coating under warm running water. Put the tomatillos in a large saucepan and cover with water by at least 2 inches. Remove the tomatillos and bring the water to a boil over high heat. Add the tomatillos and cook over high heat until the bright green skin begins to fade to pale olive, about 2 minutes. Drain the tomatillos in a colander, rinse under cold water, and set on a towel to dry. When they are cool enough to handle, cut them into ½-inch dice.

Preheat the broiler. Line a baking sheet with aluminum foil.

Quarter the poblano chiles lengthwise and remove the stems, seed cluster, and membranes. Put the chiles on the prepared baking sheet and broil until the skins are evenly blackened, 10 to 15 minutes. Immediately transfer the chiles to a small bowl and cover tightly with a pot lid, a plate, or aluminum foil. Let steam in the bowl until barely warm, about 15 minutes. Uncover and pour cold water into the bowl to loosen

ingredients that sing of the land of my youth: avocados, roasted poblano chiles, serrano chiles, and cilantro. Give me a bowl of this with some tortilla chips, and I'm one thoroughly gratified *paisano*.

Watch Alan prepare tomatillos.
youtu.be/UPNCuVb-SLU

the skins. Remove and discard the skins. If the skins prove difficult to remove in spots, just leave them on and proceed. Cut the chiles into ½-inch squares.

Put the avocado flesh in a large bowl. Add the lime juice, oil, and salt. Mash with a potato masher or a silicone spatula until almost smooth. Add the tomatillos, poblano chiles, onion, and serrano chiles and stir well. Add the cilantro and stir well. Taste and add more salt and serrano chiles if desired. Serve at once.

Per ¼ cup: 83 calories, 1 g protein, 7 g fat (1 g sat), 6 g carbohydrates, 99 mg sodium, 11 mg calcium, 4 g fiber

Go for Extraordinary! If you want to fine-tune this dish, cut the tomatillos slightly smaller than ½-inch dice. They'll blend in better—without disappearing completely—and the chances of having a chunk fall off the tortilla chip and onto your shirt will be lessened considerably. You're welcome.

avocado relish
WITH PRESERVED LEMON

See photo between pages 22 and 23.   **MAKES 2½ CUPS**

Based loosely on a guacamole theme, this condiment takes an impressive leap from Mexican cuisine. I could see it finding a home almost anywhere—not as a natural-born citizen, of course, but a welcome immigrant. I picture it showing up as a guest at a North African table or sliding easily into a forward-thinking Japanese, Thai, Persian, or Indian menu.

2 ripe avocados, cut into ½-inch dice

7 scallions, thinly sliced

⅓ cup coarsely chopped fresh cilantro leaves and tender stems, lightly packed

½ preserved lemon or lime (see page 16), cut into ¼-inch dice

2 habanero chiles, seeded and finely diced

2 tablespoons freshly squeezed lime or lemon juice

2 tablespoons extra-virgin olive oil

¼ teaspoon salt, plus more as needed

Put all the ingredients in a large bowl and gently stir with a spatula, taking care not to mash the avocado too much. Serve at once.

Per 2 tablespoons: 39 calories, 1 g protein, 4 g fat (1 g sat), 2 g carbohydrates, 30 mg sodium, 6 mg calcium, 1 g fiber

Green garbanzos have a very fresh taste, because instead of being dried, they're picked, blanched, and flash frozen all in the same day. This version of hummus is very similar in texture to conventional hummus, but I think you'll find the flavor and color spectacular. Serve this dip with carrot and celery sticks or any other cut raw vegetables.

GREEN GARBANZO hummus

MAKES 3 CUPS

2 cups frozen green garbanzo beans, thawed (see tip)

$\frac{1}{3}$ cup freshly squeezed lemon juice, plus more as needed

$\frac{1}{3}$ cup coarsely chopped fresh parsley leaves and tender stems, lightly packed

4 cloves garlic, minced or pressed

1 teaspoon sea salt, plus more as needed

1 cup tahini

$\frac{1}{4}$ cup flax oil

$\frac{1}{4}$ cup extra-virgin olive oil

Parsley sprigs, for garnish

Put the garbanzo beans in a food processor. Add the lemon juice, chopped parsley, garlic, and salt and process until smooth. With the motor running, add the tahini, followed by the flax oil and 2 tablespoons of the olive oil. Taste and add more lemon juice and salt if desired.

To serve, spread the hummus in a wide, shallow dish. Use the back of a spoon to form a trough in the surface, about 1 inch from the outside rim. Pour the remaining olive oil into the trough. Garnish with the parsley sprigs.

Per 2 tablespoons: 117 calories, 3 g protein, 10 g fat (1 g sat), 5 g carbohydrates, 123 mg sodium, 18 mg calcium, 1 g fiber

TIP If green garbanzo beans aren't available, use regular garbanzos. Even though the hummus will lack the full green color and unique flavor of the green garbanzo beans, the parsley will provide a pleasant greenish tint.

MARINATED
portobello mushrooms

Marinated mushrooms, properly made, are among the most satisfying condiments. And among condiments, they are one of the very few that also stand on their own as a side dish, a snack, or a quick salad. You can use other mushrooms, but I highly recommend portobellos for their woodsy flavor, wonderful mouthfeel, and eye appeal.

3 pounds portobello mushrooms

¼ cup extra-virgin olive oil

1 tablespoon minced garlic

2 tablespoons porcini mushroom powder (optional)

2 teaspoons sea salt

1½ teaspoons freshly ground mixed peppercorns (black, white, green, and pink)

½ teaspoon smoked paprika

4 bay leaves

1 cup water

2 tablespoons aged balsamic vinegar or Poor Man's Aged Balsamic Vinegar (page 10)

½ unsalted vegetable bouillon cube

1 small piece (about ¼ ounce) dark chocolate

½ cup finely diced red onion

¼ cup chopped fresh parsley, lightly packed

1 tablespoon chopped fresh rosemary

Wash the mushrooms and blot them dry with a towel. Carefully remove the stems by first working them back and forth to loosen them. Cut the caps into slices about ½ inch thick. Try to avoid breaking the slices.

Put 2 tablespoons of the oil in a large saucepan over medium-high heat. Add the garlic and cook for 1 minute, stirring constantly to prevent the garlic from sticking. Add the optional porcini mushroom powder, salt, pepper, paprika, and bay leaves and stir until the mixture is fragrant, about 30 seconds. Add the mushrooms, water, vinegar, and bouillon cube, and shake the saucepan back and forth briefly. Do not stir the mushrooms or they will break. Increase the heat to high and bring to a boil. Decrease the heat to medium-low, cover, and gently simmer for 2 minutes. Very gently turn the mushrooms with a silicone spatula, moving the slices at the top to the bottom. Cover and cook until all the slices have wilted slightly, about 2 minutes longer. Add the chocolate and shake the saucepan back and forth to incorporate it into the sauce. Remove from the heat and let cool to room temperature.

Add the remaining 2 tablespoons of oil and the onion, parsley, and rosemary. Toss the mushrooms and stir gently until the ingredients are thoroughly combined. Serve at room temperature. Stored in a sealed container in the refrigerator, the mushrooms will keep for 3 weeks—but why? Eat them up!

Per serving: 60 calories, 3 g protein, 4 g fat (1 g sat), 5 g carbohydrates, 168 mg sodium, 17 mg calcium, 1 g fiber

Go for Extraordinary! Although the porcini mushroom powder is optional, I highly recommend going to the trouble and the expense to obtain a small supply of this unparalleled substance. Even a teaspoon will transform a dish, elevating it well above ordinary. It doesn't spoil or lose potency the way most herbs and spices do, so you can safely assume the cost will amortize, making the mushroom powder actually quite affordable.

I'm quite fond of the entire *Allium* family, which includes onions, garlic, scallions, chives, and leeks, but certain ways of presenting them are iconic, as with this recipe. The title of this Italian dish translates roughly as "little onions in sweet-and-sour sauce," but there is more to it than that. "Cipolline" is a diminutive form of *cipolla* (onion), which refers specifically to a unique Italian variety. It's a small, flat onion, quite a bit wider than it is tall, like a cartoonishly fat coin,

cipolline IN AGRODOLCE

MAKES 4 SERVINGS

1 pound cipolline or other small onions

2 cups water

7 tablespoons aged balsamic vinegar or Poor Man's Aged
    Balsamic Vinegar (page 10)

¼ cup evaporated cane juice crystals

2 tablespoons extra-virgin olive oil

2 bay leaves

1 unsalted vegetable bouillon cube

Zest of 1 lemon

¼ teaspoon sea salt

¼ teaspoon freshly ground black pepper

Cut the roots and the tops off the cipolline onions so the tops are flush with the flat part of the bulbs, and then strip away the skin. This important step will keep the onion layers from separating during cooking so the onions remain intact. They must be peeled very patiently and carefully, so only the dry skin comes off and none of the flesh is wasted.

somewhere between an American quarter and a poker chip in diameter. Sometimes you'll see a little red onion that approximates this description, but leaning a bit in the more-round-than-flat direction and sold under the same name. Don't quibble about it, as these onions will taste just as good as the flat kind. In fact, any small onion will benefit enormously from this treatment.

Put the onions, water, vinegar, evaporated cane juice crystals, oil, bay leaves, bouillon cube, zest, salt, and pepper in a heavy pot and bring to a boil. Decrease the heat to medium-low, cover, and cook until the onions are tender and the sauce is slightly thickened, about 1½ hours. The sauce should have a consistency similar to maple syrup. Uncover occasionally to check on the onions, swirling the pot to swish them around. Do not stir with a spoon! Serve hot, warm, or at room temperature.

Per serving: 167 calories, 1 g protein, 8 g fat (2 g sat), 27 g carbohydrates, 220 mg sodium, 27 mg calcium, 1 g fiber

TIP▶ This dish can be made in advance and stored in the refrigerator for up to 1 week. Bring to room temperature or heat gently before serving.

pickled red onions
IN BLOOD ORANGE JUICE

See photo between pages 22 and 23.

I have a fondness for all citrus fruits, but blood oranges, uniquely delightful to both the eye and the palate, are by far my favorites. Keep an eye out for them when they're in season, from mid-November to early May, depending on the variety and weather conditions. Serve the pickled onions as a condiment, or drain and add them to a salad and use the liquid to build a dressing.

3 medium red onions, thinly sliced

1¼ cups blood orange juice

3 tablespoons red wine vinegar

¼ cup extra-virgin olive oil

7 cloves

2 bay leaves

1 cinnamon stick

¼ teaspoon sea salt

¼ teaspoon freshly ground
  black pepper

Put all the ingredients in a medium enamel, glass, or stainless steel saucepan and bring to a boil over high heat. Decrease the heat to medium and cook until the liquid is somewhat reduced and slightly creamy, about 5 minutes. Remove from the heat and let cool. Serve at room temperature. Stored in a covered container in the refrigerator, the onions will keep for 1 week.

Per ¼ cup: 55 calories, 1 g protein, 4 g fat (1 g sat), 5 g carbohydrates, 40 mg sodium, 6 mg calcium, 1 g fiber

Go for Extraordinary! I love Moro blood oranges for their deep, intense color and astringent, complex flavor, but I also favor the sweeter Sanguinello and Tarocco varieties. Of course, you can make this same recipe with any kind of orange and still obtain stellar results, but if you can get your hands of some dark-red blood oranges like these, you'll take this recipe over the top.

Snacks are a tricky affair. Some health experts say we should never eat between meals, and unless we aren't trying to lose weight or can carry a toothbrush everywhere we go, their argument has some merit. Others say we should eat smaller meals, and do so more frequently to keep our blood sugar from nose-diving, and perhaps they too have a point. Then there are people who just inexplicably get hungry at odd times and need to nosh on something.

There is no rule or regimen that works for all people at all times. However, there is something we can do to deflect our critics and protect ourselves from whatever they think will happen to us if we do snack between meals: we can prepare wholesome, even elegant snack options. This way, when the urge rears its head, we'll have something decent to shove in its mouth, instead of having to make due with a bag of chips or a package of unhealthful-yet-addictive cookies.

snacks

Cravings are mercurial and don't telegraph their intentions beforehand. When blood sugar plummets, you don't always have time to make a wise choice. Take control while you can, or you risk losing control when you least expect it. This chapter is about having a plan and having great options when a snack is in order. Satisfying cravings in a way that is both enjoyable and beneficial is indeed extraordinary.

grapefruit chia **DRINK**

This simple but delicious beverage is an excellent pick-me-up. Chia seeds are rich in omega-3 fatty acids, protein, and fiber, making this a "superdrink."

2 pink grapefruits, juiced
2 tablespoons chia seeds

Pour the grapefruit juice into a bowl or large glass. Add the chia seeds and stir briskly for at least 30 seconds. It's important to keep the seeds moving as they begin to absorb the juice, as this will prevent them from clumping. Let sit for 10 minutes, and then stir again. Serve at once.

Per serving: 273 calories, 8 g protein, 6 g fat (0.1 g sat), 46 g carbohydrates, 4 mg sodium, 195 mg calcium, 10 g fiber

Freshly blended green juice floods the body with health-inducing phytonutrients, fiber, enzymes, and disease-fighting antioxidants. There is no other energizing drink quite like it. Bear in mind that if you have a high-speed blender, such as a Vitamix, the results will be smoother and more palatable than those obtained with a standard blender.

HIGH-POWERED green juice

MAKES 2 SERVINGS

7 leaves Tuscan kale, center ribs removed

1 cup coarsely chopped green cabbage

2 stalks celery, sliced

1 tart apple, cored and cut into chunks

½ cucumber, sliced

¼ cup fresh mint leaves, packed (optional)

1 (1-inch) piece fresh ginger

1 (1-inch) piece fresh turmeric root (optional)

1 teaspoon matcha green tea powder (optional)

2 cups coconut water

Put all the ingredients in a high-speed blender and process until smooth. Serve at once.

Per serving: 188 calories, 4 g protein, 1 g fat (0.1 g sat), 44 g carbohydrates, 248 mg sodium, 175 mg calcium, 9 g fiber

TIP▶ Any combination of green vegetables—such as parsley, spinach, lettuce, zucchini, and green pepper—can be used. To turn this into a green high-protein drink, add your favorite protein powder (in the amount designated on the package label) while the blender is running. Matcha green tea powder contains an unusual combination of L-theanine, an amino acid that calms the mind, and caffeine, a property valued by both samurais and monks. I recommend adding it to green juice because it's also very high in antioxidants.

I've never been a fan of what I consider "fake milk," and I still don't really favor soy milk, but ever since I first tried making homemade hemp milk, I'm sold on the stuff. It's a very simple formula: one part hempseeds to two parts water, blended until smooth. If you're using it in a smoothie like this one, which includes other ingredients, just add a little more water. For an extra nutrient kick, I use coconut water, nature's own sports drink, instead of plain water.

BLUEBERRY-AÇAÍ smoothie

MAKES 1 SERVING

1½ cups coconut water

1 cup fresh or frozen blueberries

½ cup hempseeds

5 pitted medjool dates

3.5 ounces frozen unsweetened açaí purée

1 tablespoon flax oil

¼ teaspoon almond extract (optional)

Put all the ingredients in a blender and process until smooth. Serve at once.

Per serving: 430 calories, 15 g protein, 33 g fat (4 g sat), 25 g carbohydrates, 34 mg sodium, 93 mg calcium, 9 g fiber

banana-mint SMOOTHIE

Fresh mint has a cooling, relaxing effect. It's also beneficial to the digestive system.

1½ cups coconut water or water

1 banana

½ cup hempseeds

¼ cup fresh mint leaves, packed

4 pitted medjool dates

1 tablespoon flax oil (optional)

Put all the ingredients in a blender and process until smooth. Serve at once.

Per serving: 456 calories, 13 g protein, 16 g fat (2 g sat), 65 g carbohydrates, 28 mg sodium, 75 mg calcium, 7 g fiber

It's been forty years since I was in Morocco, but I still fondly remember the milk bars in Marrakech, where foreigners would gather to smoke hashish, tell tall tales, listen to rock music, and drink milkshakes. There were only three flavors—chocolate, banana, and mint—but you could also have them in combination, which was my favorite. Nothing can equal an experience of the past, especially a taste memory, but this nondairy version is far more nutritious than the milkshake of my youth, and it has the advantage of being available in the present.

CHOCOLATE-BANANA-MINT smoothie

MAKES 2 SERVINGS

1½ cups coconut water or water

1 banana

½ cup hempseeds

¼ cup raw cacao powder, or 2 tablespoons Dutch-processed cocoa

8 pitted medjool dates

2 tablespoons flax oil

1 teaspoon maca powder (optional)

¼ teaspoon peppermint extract

Put all the ingredients in a blender and process until smooth. Serve at once.

Per serving: 703 calories, 16 g protein, 27 g fat (3 g sat), 107 g carbohydrates, 35 mg sodium, 141 mg calcium, 15 g fiber

chocolate-chia SMOOTHIE

Chia is a miraculous food, no doubt about it. In addition to being high in protein, minerals, and essential fats, chia is rich in soluble fiber, which imparts a very silky texture to smoothies. One word of caution: chia thickens blended beverages very quickly, so don't stand around and talk after blending this drink, or you'll end up having to eat it with a spoon.

1¾ cups coconut water or water

2 tablespoons chia seeds

½ cup hempseeds

8 pitted medjool dates

¼ cup raw cacao powder, or
   2 tablespoons Dutch-processed cocoa

1 teaspoon maca powder (optional)

1 teaspoon vanilla extract

Put ½ cup of the coconut water in a small bowl and add the chia seeds. Whisk for about 1 minute, and then let stand for 10 minutes.

Transfer the chia mixture to a blender and add the hempseeds, dates, cacao powder, optional maca powder, and vanilla extract. Process until smooth. Serve at once.

Per serving: 691 calories, 21 g protein, 26 g fat (3 g sat), 96 g carbohydrates, 50 mg sodium, 190 mg calcium, 16 g fiber

I do a lot of hiking, biking, and outdoor exercising, which means I often find myself away from home (and kitchen) when hunger strikes. For these situations, I like to have a wholesome snack on hand. I make a habit of keeping this blend of nuts, seeds, and dried fruits in my freezer packed in small ziplock bags. When I walk out the door, they're easy to grab and take along. Each ingredient contributes a unique profile of nutrients and antioxidants, so try to include them all. However, if any prove hard to find, consider them optional. Better to leave something out than to go hungry in the wild, right?

HIGH-POTENCY trail mix

MAKES 8 SERVINGS

2 cups raw almonds

2 cups raw walnuts

1½ cups dark chocolate pieces

1 cup raw cashews

1 cup raw pumpkin seeds

1 cup raw sunflower seeds

1 cup goji berries

1 cup dried blueberries

1 cup dried mulberries

1 cup dried currants

Combine all the ingredients in a large bowl and mix thoroughly. Packed in freezer bags and stored in the freezer, the trail mix will keep indefinitely.

Per serving: 984 calories, 25 g protein, 66 g fat (11 g sat), 89 g carbohydrates, 66 mg sodium, 220 mg calcium, 17 g fiber

Go for Extraordinary! Instead of chocolate pieces, use "callets," which are small bits of high-quality chocolate available through restaurant supply outlets (see Online Shopping Sources, page 143). They look like large chocolate chips for making cookies, but that's where the similarity ends. Chocolate callets are designed to melt readily for use in recipes. Choose 70 percent cacao solids or higher for the most health benefits and lowest sugar content.

VARIATION▶ Combine 1 cup of dried black Mission figs, stems removed, and 1 cup of dried apricots in a food processor. Pulse until finely chopped. Add 1 cup of chia seeds and pulse until well mixed. Transfer to a large bowl and add all the trail mix ingredients. Using your fingers, work the chia mixture into the trail mix until it is evenly distributed. Store as directed.

NUTTY CHOCOLATE
protein bars WITH CHIA SEEDS

MAKES 12 BARS

These snacks are a lot like candy, but their sweetness comes from dates, which are high in iron and fiber, unlike refined sugar. The bars will need to be refrigerated to firm up the chocolate, but after that, they're good to go. Take them with you hiking, camping, or on a road trip. Be sure to also keep some at home for a wholesome, handy snack.

24 pitted medjool dates

1 teaspoon almond extract

⅛ teaspoon sea salt (optional)

1 cup raw almonds

½ cup raw pecans

½ cup raw walnuts

8 ounces dark chocolate, chopped or broken into small pieces

½ cup chia seeds

Put the dates, almond extract, and optional salt in a food processor and pulse until the dates are thoroughly chopped. Add the almonds, pecans, and walnuts and pulse until coarsely chopped.

Put the chocolate in a double boiler or in a small bowl set over hot, but not boiling, water. Stir the chocolate until melted. Pour the chocolate over the nut mixture in the food processor and pulse very briefly, just until combined.

Scrape the mixture onto a cutting board and form it into a square about ¾ inch thick. Cut the square into 6 strips of equal width, then cut the strips crosswise in half and separate the 12 pieces. Put the chia seeds on a small plate. Take one of the pieces and knead it slightly, warming it with your hands. Reshape it into a bar and press it into the chia seeds, coating all sides. Put the bar on a clean plate and repeat the process with the remaining pieces. Refrigerate until firm. Wrap the bars individually in plastic wrap. Stored at room temperature, the bars will keep for about 2 weeks.

Per serving: 323 calories, 7 g protein, 16 g fat (2 g sat), 43 g carbohydrates, 3 mg sodium, 125 mg calcium, 9 g fiber

This is the Lamborghini of Essene breads—and it doesn't contain any gluten! There are several steps to this recipe, and they span three days, but the actual work is relatively brief and the yield is well worth the effort. It makes a superlative traveling food, a seriously nutritious snack, and properly wrapped, a splendid gift. This is not bread to make sandwiches with, although you'll be able to spread almond butter and jam luxuriously on thick slices. This, my friends, is a bread to rightly deserve that age-old moniker "the staff of life."

HIGH-PROTEIN essene bread

MAKES 8 SMALL LOAVES (ABOUT TWELVE ½-INCH-THICK SLICES PER LOAF)

1 cup white quinoa

1 cup red quinoa or additional white quinoa

1 cup black quinoa or additional white quinoa

2 cups buckwheat groats

2 cups medium-grain brown rice

2 cups raw almonds

2 cups raw sunflower seeds

1 cup unhulled sesame seeds

2 cups raw walnuts

1 cup dried currants

2 cups grated carrots

1 cup chia seeds

½ cup golden flaxseeds

2 teaspoons sea salt

1 tablespoon extra-virgin coconut oil

Put the white, red, and black quinoa, buckwheat, and brown rice in a large bowl and mix thoroughly. Divide it equally between two one-gallon glass jars. Cover each jar with cheesecloth or similar screening material and secure it in place with a thick rubber band. Rinse the grains with cold water and then drain. Fill each jar with fresh water. Put the almonds, sunflower seeds, and sesame seeds in a separate one-gallon jar. Cover with screening material in the same way, and fill the jar with water.

Let the grains, almonds, and seeds in all three jars soak at room temperature for 8 to 12 hours. Drain and rinse the seeds and nuts, and then let them thoroughly drain by turning the jars upside down in a dish drainer.

Set the jars on their sides, away from direct light. Leave for about 8 hours, and then rinse and drain again. Let the seeds sprout for 8 to 12 hours, and then rinse, drain, and let sprout for another 8 to 12 hours.

Meanwhile, put the walnuts and currants in a medium bowl. Cover with water by at least 1 inch, and let soak at room temperature for 8 to 12 hours.

Drain but do not rinse the grains, almonds, and seeds. Drain the walnuts and currants thoroughly.

Working in batches, grind the sprouted quinoa, buckwheat, rice, sunflower seeds, almonds, and sesame seeds in a food processor to produce a dense, moist mass. Scrape the mixture into a large bowl and stir in the walnuts, currants, carrots, chia seeds, flaxseeds, and salt. Be especially careful to distribute the salt evenly.

Preheat the oven to its lowest setting. For some ovens, this could be as low as 180 degrees F. Line two baking sheets with unbleached parchment paper and coat with the coconut oil.

Divide the dough into 8 equal portions. Form each portion into a small rectangular loaf about 1½ inches thick. Put 4 of the loaves on each baking sheet. Bake for about 2½ hours, until firm when pressed lightly. Remove the baking sheets from the oven and set them on cooling racks.

While the loaves are still slightly warm, wrap them in parchment paper; this will help keep them from drying out. Once the loaves have cooled completely, wrap them tightly in an additional layer of plastic wrap or aluminum foil. The loaves will keep for 1 week in the refrigerator or 3 months in the freezer.

Per one-quarter loaf: 357 calories, 11 g protein, 20 g fat (2 g sat), 35 g carbohydrates, 190 mg sodium, 148 mg calcium, 9 g fiber

Back when I was just learning my trade, I had read and heard many times that there is no such thing as "cooking wine." A wine that is unfit to drink is unfit to eat. I found that both truthful and inspiring. This is one of those recipes that prove the point handsomely. It's an unusual, luxurious jam, not for every day, and it deserves the finest ingredients. So choose a bright, exquisite ruby port and sacrifice half the bottle upon the altar of a life well lived. Decant the rest and keep it to wash down slices of bread lavishly daubed with your freshly made jam, still slightly warm. Invite a friend. This is celebration food. Later you can snack informally on whatever is left.

fig jam WITH PORT

MAKES ABOUT 2 CUPS

2 cups dried black Mission figs, stemmed

2 cups ruby port

1 vanilla bean (optional)

Pinch sea salt

Put the figs in a small saucepan and cover with the port. If using the vanilla bean (and I strongly recommend that you do), cut it in half lengthwise with a knife. Scrape the seeds into the saucepan and add the bean. Bring to a boil over high heat. Decrease the heat to medium and simmer, uncovered, for 5 minutes. Remove from the heat, cover, and set aside until cooled completely. The liquid should be nearly all absorbed.

Drain the figs and reserve any remaining liquid. Discard the vanilla bean. Put the figs in a food processor and process into a thick paste, adding small amounts of the reserved liquid as needed to facilitate processing. Scrape into small glass jars and cover tightly. Stored in the refrigerator, the jam will keep for 3 months.

Per 2 tablespoons: 101 calories, 1 g protein, 0 g fat (0 g sat), 0 g carbohydrates, 4 mg sodium, 30 mg calcium, 3 g fiber

Ensalada de Chayote, page 72

Shaved Brussels Sprout Slaw, page 78

Edamame Salad with Penang Curry, page 81

Garbanzos with Beets, page 91

mediterranean SANDWICH SPREAD

MAKES 2 CUPS

This came together spontaneously one summer afternoon when my wife and I were working in the garden. We took a break and began rummaging through the refrigerator for a snack. I like to keep roasted peppers on hand, so that was a start. The rest came along like old friends who show up unexpectedly.

2 roasted red peppers (see page 14), **cut into ½-inch squares**

2 baby cucumbers, cut in ½-inch dice

1 avocado, cut in ½-inch dice

½ red onion, cut in ¼-inch dice

½ cup pitted kalamata olives, coarsely chopped

2 tablespoons freshly squeezed lemon juice

2 tablespoons Garlic Oil (page 9)

⅛ teaspoon sea salt

¼ teaspoon freshly ground black pepper

Put all the ingredients in a bowl and mix thoroughly but gently, taking care not to mash the avocado. Serve at once.

Per 2 tablespoons: 90 calories, 1 g protein, 8 g fat (1 g sat), 5 g carbohydrates, 208 mg sodium, 39 mg calcium, 2 g fiber

This snack requires beets with large, very fresh tops, because the leaves will be used as the wrap. Although it's a quick snack to prepare, it necessitates a little forethought, because the nuts must be soaked beforehand. Other than that, it's a snap—and a nutritious, slightly messy, eat-with-your-hands indulgence.

RAW BEET wrap

See photo facing page 23.

SERVES 2

½ cup raw almonds, soaked in water for 8 to 12 hours (see note)

½ cup raw Brazil nuts or additional almonds, soaked in water for 8 to 12 hours (see note)

¼ cup fresh basil leaves, packed

¼ teaspoon sea salt

2 tablespoons flax oil

½ cup finely diced red onion

½ cup finely diced celery hearts, including leaves

1 cup grated beets

Grated zest of 1 lemon

¼ cup Extraordinary Balsamic Vinaigrette (page 11)

8 large beet leaves, stemmed (see tip)

Drain the nuts thoroughly and put them in a food processor. Add the basil, salt, and flax oil and process into a paste. Scrape into a small bowl.

Put the onion, celery, beets, lemon zest, and balsamic vinaigrette in a medium bowl and mix well.

Hold a beet leaf in one hand, with the ribs facing down. Scoop about 1 tablespoon of the almond mixture onto the wider end of the leaf and spread it out slightly. Top with about one-eighth of the beet mixture. Roll up the leaf, enclosing the filling. Repeat with the remaining beet leaves. Serve at once.

Per serving: 844 calories, 17 g protein, 68 g fat (10 g sat), 26 g carbohydrates, 727 mg sodium, 307 mg calcium, 12 g fiber

TIP▶ Soaking nuts in cold water for several hours softens them and makes them more digestible. If you're in a hurry, you can pour boiling water over the nuts and let them soak for just 1 hour. The first method is preferable because nuts contain fragile fats that don't tolerate heat very well, but the second will work in a pinch.

VARIATION▶ If the beets don't have fresh, usable greens, use Swiss chard or lettuce leaves for the wraps.

In the old days, a soup was the whole meal. In fact, the word "supper" comes from the word "soup." I heard this as a kid from my father, who was a learned fount of odd bits of marginally useful information. We used to eat our main meal in the middle of the day, and then we'd usually have soup and toast for dinner. Canned soup, that is, with a dash of a bottled condiment to "doctor it up," as my mother would say. I didn't know it then, but those canned soups were beyond doctoring. They had nothing in common with the soups of yore that gave supper its name. Those were complex, nourishing soups like the ones that bubbled nonstop in cauldrons over hearth fires in French farmhouses, and to which fresh vegetables and herbs were added each day to keep them going.

soups

In our time, it would be asking a little too much of the average home cook to start with homemade stocks and build up an old-country European-style soup. But there is a lot we can do now that was close to impossible in my great-grandmother's time. We don't have to chop wood and build a fire in the stove, or push cooked vegetables through a sieve to purée them. Our machines and tools make quick work of tasks that once took hours. And we have access to products our grandparents had never heard of. In virtually any city, we can find ingredients from the cuisines of faraway lands and use them traditionally or heretically, as the mood strikes us. What an exciting time to be alive!

Very often, basil is associated with tomatoes—and it is a match made in culinary heaven—but it also does zucchini a world of good. This soup all but cries out to be made in the summer, when both zucchini and basil are at their peak. The variation with mint, a close cousin of basil, is another perfect summer match.

zucchini soup WITH BASIL

MAKES 4 SERVINGS

3 tablespoons extra-virgin olive oil

1 white onion, diced

4 zucchini, diced

4 cloves garlic, minced or pressed

4 cups water

2 unsalted vegetable bouillon cubes

¼ teaspoon sea salt

¼ cup fresh basil leaves, packed

Freshly ground black pepper

1 tablespoon basil microgreens or torn fresh basil leaves, for garnish

Heat the oil in a large soup pot over medium-high heat until fragrant, about 30 seconds. Add the onion and cook, stirring often, until it begins to soften, about 3 minutes. Add the zucchini and garlic and cook, stirring almost constantly, until the mixture is nearly dry but not browned, about 3 minutes.

Add the water, bouillon cubes, and salt. Increase the heat to high and bring to a boil. Decrease the heat to medium-low and cook, uncovered, until the vegetables are very tender, about 10 minutes.

Transfer to a blender and add the basil. Process until smooth. Return to the pot and season with pepper to taste. Reheat. Serve at once, garnished with the basil microgreens.

Per serving: 140 calories, 3 g protein, 11 g fat (2 g sat), 10 g carbohydrates, 186 mg sodium, 91 mg calcium, 3 g fiber

TIP▶ On a hot day, this soup is delicious served cold. The microgreens will hold up even better this way, as they will not wilt.

VARIATION▶ Replace the basil with 2 tablespoons chopped fresh mint and 2 tablespoons chopped chives. Mint or chive microgreens would be an excellent garnish for this variation, but they're rather difficult to find. Snipped chives or thinly sliced mint leaves—or a little of each—would be just as flavorful.

I love green soups—green anything, actually. But when it comes to kale, I much prefer to eat it raw so I can take advantage of every bit of the enzyme and phytonutrient content. This hybrid soup combines the best of both worlds—cooked and raw. This recipe makes eight servings: four to eat hot and four to eat cold the following day.

GREEN GARBANZO
AND FRESH KALE soup

MAKES 8 SERVINGS

1 tablespoon extra-virgin olive oil

3 cups diced onion

4 cloves garlic, minced

½ teaspoon sea salt, plus more as needed

4 cups frozen green garbanzo beans, peas, edamame, or a combination, thawed

8 cups water

3 unsalted vegetable bouillon cubes

10 leaves Tuscan kale, center ribs removed

2 tablespoons freshly squeezed lemon juice

⅛ teaspoon ground mace or freshly grated nutmeg, plus more for garnish

Heat the oil in a large soup pot over medium-high heat until fragrant, about 30 seconds. Add the onion and cook, stirring frequently, until it begins to soften, about 2 minutes. Add the garlic and salt and cook, stirring frequently, for 2 minutes longer. Add the garbanzo beans, water, and bouillon cubes. Increase the heat to high and bring to a boil. Decrease the heat to medium-low, and cook until the vegetables are tender, about 10 minutes.

Chop the kale coarsely and put it in a blender. Pour the contents of the soup pot on top of the kale and process until smooth and bright green. Strain the soup and stir in the lemon juice and mace. Serve at once, garnished with a pinch of mace in the center.

Per serving: 197 calories, 14 g protein, 8 g fat (2 g sat), 18 g carbohydrates, 229 mg sodium, 123 mg calcium, 7 g fiber

TIP▶ If you prefer, after the soup has been blended, reheat it over low heat, stirring constantly. This soup is also delicious served cold, with an additional tablespoon or two of freshly squeezed lemon juice stirred in just before serving.

VARIATION▶ Add ¼ cup of fresh basil leaves, packed, along with the kale. Omit the nutmeg, and garnish with basil microgreens if available.

When I was in Peru, I was surprised to learn that, unlike Mexicans, who enjoy having their mouths set on fire, Peruvians prefer a slightly milder bite, with more subtlety of flavor. Years later, quite by chance, I found two very unique Peruvian chiles, aji amarillo and aji panca, at a spice shop in Colorado Springs, of all places.

red pepper soup
WITH GRILLED CORN

MAKES 4 SERVINGS

4 ears white corn, shucked and silk removed

3 tablespoons extra-virgin olive oil

1 large yellow onion, diced

7 cloves garlic, minced

6 Roasted Red Peppers (page 14), diced

2 teaspoons panca chile or Hungarian hot paprika

2 teaspoons amarillo chile, or ½ teaspoon red chile powder

½ teaspoon sea salt

½ teaspoon smoked paprika

4 cups water

2 unsalted vegetable bouillon cubes

2 bay leaves

¼ teaspoon freshly ground black pepper, plus more as needed

4 thin scallions, very thinly sliced

Preheat a gas or charcoal grill (see tip) and put the corn on it. Turn the corn as needed to char the surface evenly, about 10 minutes. Don't worry if it appears to be badly burned in spots; the flavor imparted will be very agreeable when combined with the other ingredients. When the corn is evenly charred, wrap in a sheet of foil and let

Roasted peppers, grilled corn, and smoked paprika make an alluring blend, but with the addition of these two exotic chiles, I obtained a complex flavor profile that performed a lively dance. Feel free to insert any combination of distinctive chiles you deem appropriate, or substitute with the suggestions below.

steam in the residual heat until cool enough to handle. Unwrap and cut the kernels off the cobs into a large bowl.

Heat the oil in a large soup pot over medium-high heat until fragrant, about 30 seconds. Add the onion and cook, stirring often, until it begins to soften, about 3 minutes. Add the garlic and roasted peppers and cook, stirring almost constantly, until nearly dry, about 5 minutes. Add the panca chile, amarillo chile, salt, and smoked paprika, and stir to mix well. Add the water, bouillon cubes, and bay leaves and stir well. Increase the heat to high and bring to a boil. Decrease the heat to medium and simmer until the vegetables are very tender, about 20 minutes. Remove and discard the bay leaves.

Transfer the contents of the pot to a blender and process until smooth. Return to the pot and add the reserved corn and pepper. Stir well. Taste and add more pepper if desired. Reheat the soup over medium heat until steaming. Serve at once, garnished with the scallions.

Per serving: 274 calories, 6 g protein, 13 g fat (3 g sat), 44 g carbohydrates, 744 mg sodium, 283 mg calcium, 5 g fiber

TIP▶ A grill will create the best flavor for the corn. However, if you don't have a grill, you can "grill" the corn by placing it on the flame of a gas stove or, as a last resort, under a broiler.

A VERY DIFFERENT
butternut squash soup

I'm an avid fan of all winter squashes, and butternut squash is among my favorites. However, I've found that almost all butternut squash soups tend to taste alike, so I endeavored to make a version that's both unique and extraordinary. This exceptional rendition includes roasted peppers, smoked paprika, and saffron, and I think you'll find it uncommonly delicious.

3 tablespoons extra-virgin coconut oil

1 large yellow onion, diced

12 cloves garlic, minced

4 Roasted Red Peppers (page 14), diced

1 small butternut squash, peeled and diced (about 4 cups)

2 small yams, peeled and diced (about 3 cups)

1 teaspoon sea salt

½ teaspoon smoked paprika

8 cups water

3 unsalted vegetable bouillon cubes

4 bay leaves

Pinch of saffron (optional; see note)

½ teaspoon hot red chile powder

Freshly ground black pepper

1 tablespoon snipped chives, for garnish

Heat the oil in a large soup pot over high heat until fragrant, about 30 seconds. Add the onions and stir until they begin to soften, about 3 minutes. Decrease the heat to medium-high and add the garlic. Cook, stirring constantly, until the vegetables are nearly dry, about 4 minutes. Add the roasted peppers and cook, stirring frequently, for 2 minutes. Add the squash, yams, salt, and smoked paprika, and stir to mix well. Add the water, bouillon cubes, and bay leaves. Increase the heat to high and bring to a boil. Decrease the heat to medium and simmer until the vegetables are very tender, about 25 minutes. Remove and discard the bay leaves.

Working in batches, transfer the contents of the pot to a blender and process until smooth. Strain the soup into a clean soup pot and add the optional saffron and hot chile powder. Season with pepper to taste. Reheat over medium heat, stirring often to prevent scorching. Serve at once, garnished with the chives.

Per serving: 184 calories, 3 g protein, 7 g fat (6 g sat), 32 g carbohydrates, 481 mg sodium, 194 mg calcium, 3 g fiber

Go for Extraordinary! Although the saffron is optional, I highly recommend including it. Saffron is fairly expensive, but it only takes a very small amount to do the job. In this recipe, it adds a near-transcendental layer of flavor and elevates the dish to truly exceptional heights. Once you start using saffron, you're bound to become addicted to it, as I am.

curried pea and lettuce soup

Lettuce has been grilled, braised, and made into soup in French cooking for a long time. Although the traditional version of lettuce soup includes quite a bit of cream, I've discovered that the texture achieved by the puréed peas alone provides more than enough creaminess without adding any dairy products.

SOUP

2 tablespoons extra-virgin coconut oil

1 large white onion, thinly sliced

2 cloves garlic, coarsely chopped

1 large head romaine lettuce, coarsely chopped

1 tablespoon curry powder

½ teaspoon sea salt, plus more as needed

4 cups water

2 unsalted vegetable bouillon cubes

1 pound frozen peas

1½ cups coarsely chopped fresh Italian parsley leaves and tender stems, lightly packed

¼ teaspoon freshly ground black pepper

To make the soup, heat the coconut oil in a large soup pot over medium-high heat until fragrant, about 30 seconds. Add the onion and garlic and cook, stirring constantly, until the onion begins to soften, about 5 minutes. Add the lettuce and cook, stirring constantly, until it wilts, 1 to 2 minutes. Add the curry powder and salt and cook, stirring constantly, until the mixture is thoroughly combined and nearly dry, about 2 minutes. Add the water and bouillon cubes. Increase the heat to high and bring to a boil. Add the peas and parsley and return to a boil. Decrease the heat to medium and simmer, uncovered, until the peas are very tender, about 15 minutes.

Remove from the heat and let cool slightly. Working in batches, process in a blender until smooth. Strain into a clean soup pot and reheat over medium heat until steaming hot. Stir in the pepper. Taste and add more salt if desired.

WITH TEMPEH CROUTONS

CROUTONS

¼ cup extra-virgin coconut oil, plus more
   as needed

8 ounces tempeh, cut into ½-inch squares

While the soup is cooking, make the croutons. Heat the coconut oil in a small skillet and add a few tempeh pieces, without crowding. Fry on one side until golden brown, about 2 minutes. Turn them over and brown the other side, about 2 minutes. Remove from the pan with a slotted spoon and drain on a paper towel, blotting with a second paper towel. Repeat with the remaining tempeh, adding more coconut oil if needed.

Ladle the soup into shallow soup bowls. Serve at once, passing a bowl of the croutons separately.

Per serving: 431 calories, 18 g protein, 24 g fat (20 g sat), 33 g carbohydrates, 499 mg sodium, 151 mg calcium, 15 g fiber

three sisters SOUP

MAKES 4 SERVINGS

Lyrically named, the "three sisters" refers to the cornerstones of the Mesoamerican diet: corn, beans, and squash. This recipe isn't difficult to prepare, but the result is quite complex and satisfying. If you can't find the specific chiles listed, substitute with the most interesting and flavorful chiles you have available, such as chipotle, smoked serrano, hot paprika, or Aleppo pepper, to name just a few.

2 tablespoons extra-virgin coconut oil

1 large yellow onion, diced

2 stalks celery, diced

1 red pepper, diced

2 cups peeled and diced kabocha or butternut squash

12 cloves garlic, minced or pressed

6 cups water

3 unsalted vegetable bouillon cubes

½ teaspoon sea salt, plus more as needed

1 teaspoon ground guajillo chile or ancho chile (optional)

1 teaspoon ground amarillo chile or panca chile (optional)

1 teaspoon smoked paprika

3 ears fresh white corn, or 2 cups frozen white corn

2 cups cooked black beans, or 1 can (16 ounces) no-salt-added black beans, drained and rinsed

⅓ cup freshly squeezed lime juice

1 cup coarsely chopped fresh cilantro leaves and tender stems, lightly packed

Sriracha sauce (optional)

Heat the oil in a large soup pot over medium-high heat until fragrant, about 30 seconds. Add the onion and cook, stirring almost constantly, until it begins to soften, about 2 minutes. Add the celery and red pepper and cook, stirring frequently, until they begin to soften, about 2 minutes. Add the squash and garlic and stir well. Decrease the heat to medium-low, cover, and cook, stirring occasionally, until the vegetables are soft and very fragrant, about 10 minutes.

Add the water, bouillon cubes, salt, optional guajillo chile, optional amarillo chile, and smoked paprika, stirring well. Increase the heat to high and bring to a boil. Cut the corn kernels off the cobs directly into the pot. Scrape the remaining starch off the cobs with the back of the knife and add to the pot. Stir until any clumps of kernels have broken up. Decrease the heat to medium and simmer until all the vegetables are tender, about 20 minutes. Stir in the beans and heat through. Taste and add more salt if desired. Remove from the heat and stir in the lime juice and cilantro. Serve at once, passing sriracha sauce on the side if desired.

Per serving: 277 calories, 5 g protein, 10 g fat (9 g sat), 44 g carbohydrates, 102 mg sodium, 46 mg calcium, 6 g fiber

Go for Extraordinary! For even more extraordinary flavor and texture, pass a bowl of diced avocado at the table as an additional garnish.

Huitlacoche, or "corn smut," is a fungus that infects and grows on ears of corn. It has been a delicacy in Mexico since pre-Columbian times, although it has never made it into mainstream gourmet circles, even after James Beard dubbed it the "Mexican truffle." This is probably due to huitlacoche's considerably off-putting appearance—an inky-black goop with gnarled, gray,

corn, potato, and leek soup
WITH HUITLACOCHE

MAKES 4 SERVINGS .

2 tablespoons extra-virgin olive oil

1 large leek, white part only, thinly sliced

1 small white onion, thinly sliced

2 cloves garlic, coarsely chopped

8 cups water

1½ pounds russet potatoes, peeled and thinly sliced

2 cups white corn kernels

2 unsalted vegetable bouillon cubes

½ teaspoon sea salt, plus more as needed

1 can (7 ounces) huitlacoche

1 teaspoon finely chopped epazote (optional)

1½ tablespoons chopped fresh cilantro leaves

1 lime, quartered

Heat the oil in a large soup pot over medium heat until fragrant, about 30 seconds. Add the leek, onion, and garlic and stir well. Shake the pot to spread the vegetables into an even layer, cover, and decrease the heat to low. Let the vegetables sweat for 15 minutes, checking them occasionally. If the vegetables start to stick to the pot, add 1 tablespoon of water.

swollen corn kernels interspersed with odd bits of corn silk. I know that sounds awful, but like truffles, this stuff will definitely grow on you (not literally, of course). Look for huitlacoche in cans and fresh epazote at Mexican markets. If you don't find any, don't let that stop you; even without them, this is still a great soup!

Add the 8 cups of water and bring to a boil over high heat. Add the potatoes, corn, bouillon cubes, and salt and return to a boil. Decrease the heat to medium, cover, and simmer until the potatoes are very tender, about 25 minutes. Remove from the heat and let cool slightly. Working in batches, process the vegetables in a blender until smooth. Strain into a clean pot. Reheat over medium heat until steaming hot. Taste and add more salt if desired.

Put the huitlacoche in a small bowl and stir in the optional epazote.

To serve, ladle the soup into shallow soup bowls and put 1 tablespoon of the huitlacoche in the center. Swirl into the soup decoratively with the tip of a knife, and then add another tablespoon of the huitlacoche, again in the center. Garnish with the cilantro. Put a lime wedge on the rim of each bowl and serve at once.

Per serving: 338 calories, 6 g protein, 9 g fat (2 g sat), 55 g carbohydrates, 637 mg sodium, 67 mg calcium, 7 g fiber

ROASTED JERUSALEM
artichoke soup

MAKES 4 SERVINGS

The first time I ever cooked Jerusalem artichokes—which have nothing whatsoever to do with Jerusalem *or* artichokes, by the way—I used an Italian recipe that set a high standard for preparing this unique vegetable. It called for slicing the starchy tubers very thinly, prior to sautéing them in olive oil with thinly sliced garlic. Slow cooking, with a relentless turning of the vegetables, produces a lightly caramelized dish of unparalleled flavor. Every time I've approached Jerusalem artichokes since, I've begun the same way, in order to achieve the same underlying flavor base. You're going to love this.

3 tablespoons extra-virgin olive oil

1½ pounds Jerusalem artichokes, peeled and thinly sliced

7 cloves garlic, thinly sliced

½ teaspoon sea salt

4 cups water

1 unsalted vegetable bouillon cube

1 tablespoon dry sherry

1 tablespoon snipped chives

Preheat the oven to 475 F.

Heat the oil in a large ovenproof skillet over high heat until fragrant, about 30 seconds. Add the Jerusalem artichokes, garlic, and salt and cook, stirring constantly, until the vegetables are thoroughly coated with the oil and begin to color lightly, about 7 minutes. Put the skillet in the oven and roast, stirring frequently to prevent burning, until the vegetables are tender and lightly browned, about 30 minutes.

Transfer the vegetables to a large soup pot. Add the water and bouillon cube and bring to a boil over high heat. Decrease the heat to medium, cover, and simmer until the vegetables are very tender, about 15 minutes. Remove from the heat and let cool slightly.

Process in batches in blender until smooth. Strain into a clean soup pot and reheat over medium-low heat, stirring frequently to prevent scorching, until steaming hot. Stir in the sherry. Serve at once, garnished with the chives.

Per serving: 373 calories, 7 g protein, 11 g fat (2 g sat), 63 g carbohydrates, 347 mg sodium, 143 mg calcium, 6 g fiber

CHAPTER 7

I often say, "When it comes to food, vegan is the highest common denominator," because everyone eats plants. I said this to someone at a vegetarian festival once, and he immediately came back with, "Actually, *raw* vegan is." Apparently he ate only raw food, and he wanted to set the bar higher. Fair enough. I conceded the point, although I remember thinking to myself, having grown up in a developing country, that eating raw food isn't always the best option. Although consuming certain foods in their raw state may be a good way to take advantage of all they have to offer nutritionally, sometimes uncooked food harbors unfriendly microorganisms.

salads

But the fact remains that raw food in a high proportion is a must for optimum health, and salads are the easiest, most enjoyable way to get our quota. Almost limitless variety is possible with the array of vegetables, herbs, fruits, nuts, and seeds at our disposal. We could probably eat a different salad every day for a year. And that would be a healthful project, because each plant has a unique profile of phytonutrients, enzymes, antioxidants, and medicinal qualities. The more we vary our diets by including a substantial amount of raw foods, the more we make use of all of these valuable components.

This salad is fantastic for picnics, as it remains delicious for a couple of days. Even though chayotes are fairly bland, their unique flavor is potent enough to shine through a riot of assertive players, like the grilled corn, chiles, garlic, onion, and cilantro in this dish. Don't be intimidated by the length of this recipe, as several steps can be done concurrently.

ensalada DE CHAYOTE

See photo facing page 54.

MAKES 10 SERVINGS

4 ears white corn, shucked and silk removed

4 large poblano chiles, quartered, seeds and membranes removed

2 large unblemished chayotes

6 tomatillos, dry skin removed

3 stalks celery, diced

1 large red onion, finely diced

1 small jicama, peeled and cut in ½-inch dice (about 2 cups)

2 cups coarsely chopped fresh cilantro leaves, packed

2 serrano chiles, finely diced, plus more as needed (optional)

7 cloves garlic, peeled

⅓ cup freshly squeezed lime juice

⅓ cup extra-virgin olive oil

1½ teaspoons sea salt

¼ teaspoon freshly ground black pepper

3 large avocados, cut into ½-inch dice

1 pound mixed baby lettuce, washed and spun dry (optional)

Preheat a gas or charcoal grill (see tip) on high and put the corn on it. Turn the corn as needed to char the surface evenly, about 10 minutes. Don't worry if the corn appears to be badly burned in spots; the flavor imparted will be very agreeable when combined with the other ingredients. Wrap the charred corn in a sheet of foil and let steam in the residual heat until cool enough to handle. Unwrap and cut the kernels off the cobs into a large bowl.

Preheat a broiler.

Put the poblano chiles on a baking sheet, as close together as possible without touching. Broil the chiles until lightly blackened, about 10 minutes. Immediately slip the chiles into a bowl of cold water to stop the cooking. After 2 minutes, remove and discard the charred skins. Put 4 of the poblano quarters in a blender and set aside. Cut the remaining pieces into ½-inch squares and add to the bowl of corn.

Bring a large pot of water to a boil and add the chayotes and tomatillos. Return to a boil and cook until the tomatillos turn an olive color and are slightly tender, 2 to 3 minutes. Remove the tomatillos with a slotted spoon and put them in the blender with the poblano chiles. Continue cooking the chayotes until just tender, 18 to 22 minutes longer. If you insert a paring knife into them and lift, they should slide off slowly. Drain the chayotes and put them in a bowl of cold water until cool enough to handle. Peel them, cut them in half lengthwise, and cut out the tough core. Eat the flat "almond" in the center (it's every cook's secret prerogative) and cut the chayotes into ½-inch dice. Add to the corn mixture along with the celery, onion, jicama, three-quarters of the cilantro, and the optional serrano chiles.

Put the remaining cilantro in the blender. Add the garlic, lime juice, olive oil, salt, and pepper. Process until smooth. Pour over the vegetables in the bowl and toss thoroughly. Add the avocados and gently toss again, taking care not to mash the avocado pieces. Serve the salad on beds of the lettuce, if using, or in bowls.

Per serving: 247 calories, 4 g protein, 15 g fat (2 g sat), 28 g carbohydrates, 363 mg sodium, 72 mg calcium, 12 g fiber

TIP▶ A grill will create the best flavor for the corn. However, if you don't have a grill, you can "grill" the corn by placing it on the flame of a gas stove or, as a last resort, under a broiler.

white asparagus salad
WITH SHERRY VINAIGRETTE

MAKES 4 SERVINGS

White asparagus is a seasonal vegetable, appearing in middle to late spring. It can be somewhat expensive, so consider this salad a special treat. White asparagus looks a little anemic compared to its green cousin, but its flavor is beyond compare. Unlike green asparagus, white asparagus is cultivated underground, with dirt piled up around the stalks as they grow upward. It's a European thing. This salad makes a perfect first course for an elegant meal.

2 pounds white asparagus

2¼ teaspoons sea salt

3 tablespoons sherry vinegar

1 teaspoon Dijon mustard

¼ teaspoon freshly ground black pepper

7 tablespoons walnut oil

2 teaspoons white truffle oil (optional)

4 teaspoons snipped chives

Put the asparagus spears side by side on a cutting board, four or five at a time, with the tips lined up evenly. Holding the group firmly with one hand, cut the coarse ends off in a straight line. Repeat with the remaining asparagus, using one of the cut spears as a guide to ensure equal length. Starting just below the flowering tips, remove the tough skin with a vegetable peeler. Wash the tips carefully, dislodging any embedded dirt, and then put the asparagus in a large bowl of cold water.

Fill a large pot with water, add 2 teaspoons of the salt, and bring to a boil over high heat. Lift the asparagus out of the bowl of water and put them in the boiling water. Cook until they are just tender, 2 to 4 minutes. The exact time will depend on their freshness and thickness. While the asparagus are cooking, prepare a large bowl of cold water with ice. Lift the asparagus out with tongs, taking care to avoid bruising them, and put them in the ice water. Then drain and spread the asparagus out on a clean towel. Pat them dry with another towel.

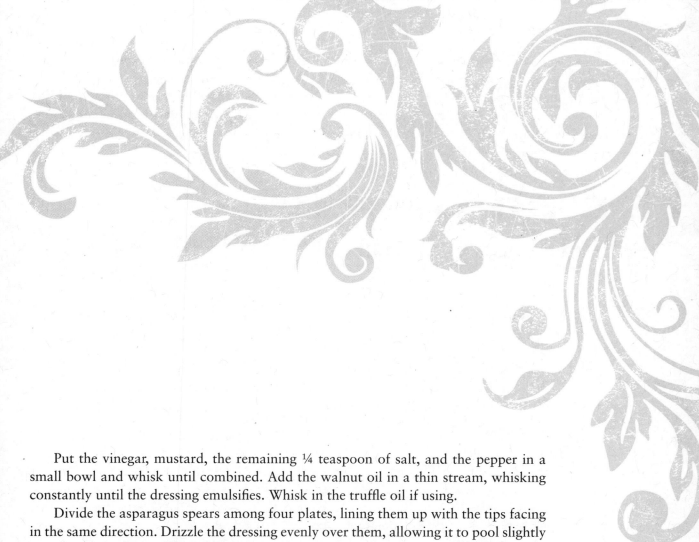

Put the vinegar, mustard, the remaining ¼ teaspoon of salt, and the pepper in a small bowl and whisk until combined. Add the walnut oil in a thin stream, whisking constantly until the dressing emulsifies. Whisk in the truffle oil if using.

Divide the asparagus spears among four plates, lining them up with the tips facing in the same direction. Drizzle the dressing evenly over them, allowing it to pool slightly on the plates. Strew the chives elegantly over the asparagus and serve at once.

Per serving: 275 calories, 5 g protein, 25 g fat (2 g sat), 12 g carbohydrates, 308 mg sodium, 51 mg calcium, 5 g fiber

Go for Extraordinary! Truffle oil elevates the flavor of this salad significantly.
Although it's a little pricey, it only takes a small amount of truffle oil to infuse an entire dish. Since you probably will use this oil only occasionally, you can keep it fresh for several months by storing it in the freezer. Simply thaw the oil by placing the bottle in a large glass of warm water for a few minutes before using. Afterward, seal the bottle tightly and return it to the freezer.

I don't generally favor prewashed bagged salad greens. So often you end up having to pick through the mixture and pull out a bunch of bruised and rotten bits, which can sometimes end up being half the bag. However, I will occasionally make an exception for very fresh Asian greens, primarily because it's the only way to find them where I live. With their unique combination of textures and flavors—a little bitter, with some astringent notes—they offer a thoroughly enjoyable salad experience.

asian greens
WITH BEAN SPROUTS AND MANGOES

MAKES 4 SERVINGS

5 ounces mixed Asian greens

8 ounces bean sprouts

3 Roasted Red Peppers (page 14),
    sliced into ¾-inch-wide strips

2 ripe mangoes, cut into ¾-inch dice

10 scallions, sliced on a sharp
    diagonal

2 cloves garlic, minced or pressed

¼ cup freshly squeezed lime juice

1 tablespoon reduced-sodium tamari

1 tablespoon sriracha sauce

½ teaspoon toasted sesame oil

1 tablespoon black sesame seeds

Put the greens in a large bowl of cold water. Add the bean sprouts, agitate gently, and let soak for 15 to 20 minutes. Drain and then dry in a salad spinner. Transfer to a large bowl and add the roasted peppers and mangoes. Set aside about one-quarter of the scallions to use as a garnish and add the rest to the bowl.

Put the garlic in a small bowl. Add the lime juice, tamari, sriracha sauce, and sesame oil and whisk until well combined (it will not emulsify). Pour over the vegetables and mango and toss gently but thoroughly.

Divide the salad among four plates. Garnish with the reserved scallions and a sprinkling of the sesame seeds. Serve at once.

Per serving: 131 calories, 5 g protein, 3 g fat (0.3 g sat), 30 g carbohydrates, 448 mg sodium, 201 mg calcium, 5 g fiber

Go for Extraordinary! Look for champagne mangoes, as they have incredibly sweet, velvety flesh and a wafer-thin pit.

watercress salad
WITH ROASTED GOLDEN BEETS

Roasting enhances the sweetness of beets and concentrates their flavor. To keep the spotlight on the beets and the bright, sharp flavor of the watercress, I kept the dressing for this salad and the other ingredients as unobtrusive as possible; the only additions are a shallot and walnuts. This salad should thrill your entire palate.

3 medium golden beets, scrubbed and quartered lengthwise

3½ tablespoons walnut oil

½ teaspoon sea salt

½ teaspoon freshly ground black pepper

2 bunches watercress (about 5 cups)

1½ tablespoons sherry vinegar

1 teaspoon Dijon mustard

1 shallot, finely diced

1 cup walnut halves

Preheat the oven to 375 degrees F.

Put the beets in a medium bowl. Sprinkle with 1 tablespoon of the oil, ¼ teaspoon of the salt, and ¼ teaspoon of the pepper. Toss until the oil and seasonings are evenly distributed. Transfer the beets to a 13 x 9-inch baking dish and spread them in a single layer. Bake for 40 minutes, stirring every 10 minutes to ensure even browning, until the beets are tender and lightly browned. Remove from the oven and let cool. Cut the beets crosswise into ½-inch-thick slices .

While the beets are roasting, pick over the watercress and remove any coarse stems and bruised leaves. Put the watercress in a bowl of cool water and let soak until the beets are cool. Drain and spin dry or wrap very gently in a towel.

Put the remaining oil, salt, and pepper in a large bowl. Add the vinegar and mustard and whisk until emulsified. Add the beets, shallot, and watercress. Toss very gently but thoroughly. Add the walnuts and toss again. Divide the salad among 4 plates and serve at once.

Per serving: 327 calories, 6 g protein, 30 g fat (3 g sat), 11 g carbohydrates, 366 mg sodium, 81 mg calcium, 4 g fiber

My friendship with Brussels sprouts has always been predicated on specific methods of preparation. One day the kitchen gods whispered to me, "They're little cabbages, so why not make them into a coleslaw?" I listened to their advice and cut the Brussels sprouts into paper-thin shavings (a mandoline made quick, easy work of this) and added only a little red cabbage and grated carrot. I didn't want to take any chances with the flavor, so I enveloped everything in a potent dressing. This is one outrageously delectable hot-sweet-sour-pungent-creamy tangle of crunchiness. And the colors! Wait till you see the colors!

shaved
BRUSSELS SPROUT SLAW

See photo between pages 54 and 55. MAKES 4 SERVINGS

4 cups Brussels sprouts

¼ head red cabbage, cored and very thinly sliced

1 large carrot, finely shredded

6 tablespoons freshly squeezed lime juice

¼ cup flax oil

3 tablespoons sherry vinegar

2 tablespoons raw cashew butter or almond butter

2 tablespoons mellow white miso

1 tablespoon reduced-sodium tamari

4 cloves garlic, minced or pressed

2 teaspoons sriracha sauce

2 teaspoons grated fresh ginger

Peel off any wilted or discolored leaves from the Brussels sprouts. Beginning with the top, slice the Brussels sprouts as thinly as possible, discarding the stem end. Put the Brussels sprouts in a large bowl. Add the red cabbage and carrot and fluff with your fingers until the vegetables are thoroughly mixed.

Put the lime juice, flax oil, vinegar, cashew butter, miso, tamari, garlic, sriracha, and ginger in a small bowl and whisk until smooth and well combined. Pour over the vegetables and toss well. Serve at once.

Per serving: 423 calories, 17 g protein, 18 g fat (2 g sat), 58 g carbohydrates, 705 mg sodium, 300 mg calcium, 17 g fiber

TIP▶ If you're not a fan of spicy food, you can cut back or omit the sriracha sauce with no serious consequences to the flavor of the dressing.

QUICK spicy slaw

This salad is a simple blend of harmonies and counterpoints, colors and textures. It delights the eye, the palate, and the entire digestive system.

½ cup Garlic Oil (page 9)

¼ cup freshly squeezed lime juice

3 tablespoons mellow white miso

1 tablespoon grated fresh ginger

2 teaspoons sriracha sauce

1 cup grated beets

1 cup grated carrots

1 cup thinly sliced red cabbage

½ large fennel bulb, sliced

½ red onion, sliced

Put the oil, lime juice, miso, ginger, and sriracha sauce in a medium bowl and whisk until thoroughly combined. Add the beets, carrots, cabbage, fennel, and onion and toss well. Serve at once.

Per serving: 338 calories, 3 g protein, 29 g fat (4 g sat), 20 g carbohydrates, 569 mg sodium, 70 mg calcium, 3 g fiber

SPICY minted SLAW

This slaw is free of extracted oils but bursting with flavor. If you can find fresh turmeric root, by all means use it. If not, ask your natural food market to order it. Fresh turmeric not only has a uniquely interesting taste, but it's also among the most potent anti-inflammatory, anticancer, anti-everything-that-ails-you foods on Earth.

1 medium napa cabbage, thinly sliced

7 large leaves Tuscan kale, center ribs removed and thinly sliced

1 red pepper, cut lengthwise into thin strips

10 scallions, thinly sliced on a sharp diagonal

1 can (14.5 ounces) full-fat coconut milk

1 cup fresh mint leaves, packed

¼ cup freshly squeezed lime juice

2 tablespoons grated fresh ginger

2 cloves garlic

¼ teaspoon sea salt

3 tablespoons raw almond butter

4 green chiles, finely diced, plus more as needed (optional)

1 (3-inch) piece fresh turmeric root (optional)

Put the cabbage, kale, red pepper, and half the scallions in a large bowl and toss until well combined. Fingers do the best job of this, if no one is looking, but tongs will do in a pinch.

Put the coconut milk, mint, lime juice, ginger, garlic, and salt in a blender and process until smooth. Add the almond butter and process until well incorporated. Pour over the vegetables in the bowl and toss until evenly distributed. Divide among 6 plates. Top with the optional chiles and remaining scallions. Finely grate the turmeric root, if using, directly over each salad. Serve at once.

Per serving: 337 calories, 9 g protein, 25 g fat (15 g sat), 24 g carbohydrates, 199 mg sodium, 156 mg calcium, 7 g fiber

TIP This salad is satisfying enough for a whole meal, but you may instead choose to serve this as part of a multicourse meal. In that case, it will serve 6 to 8 people, depending on the courses that precede and follow it.

Penang curry is my all-time favorite in the Thai constellation of sublime dishes. Although using Thai curry paste in a salad dressing is a nontraditional application, I like it for its unique flavor profile and mild but assertive heat. This is a salad with just about everything you need in one meal: protein, essential fats, fiber, complex carbohydrates, and, most important of all, enjoyment!

edamame salad
WITH PENANG CURRY

See photo between pages 54 and 55.   **MAKES 4 SERVINGS**

1 pound frozen edamame

2 cups thinly sliced celery with leaves

1 large carrot, grated

10 scallions, sliced thinly on a sharp diagonal

1 red bell pepper, cut into thin strips

1 cup coarsely chopped fresh cilantro leaves and tender stems, lightly packed

⅓ cup flax oil

¼ cup freshly squeezed lime juice

3 tablespoons mellow white miso

2 tablespoons raw tahini

2 tablespoons Penang curry paste or red curry paste

1 tablespoon grated fresh ginger

1 tablespoon Roasted Garlic (page 12)

2 avocados, cut into ½-inch dice

Fill a large saucepan with water and bring to a boil over high heat. Add the edamame. As soon as the water returns to a boil, drain the edamame in a colander and refresh under cold running water. Drain thoroughly and set aside until cooled completely.

Put the edamame, celery, carrot, scallions, and bell pepper in a large bowl. Set aside ¼ cup of the cilantro and add the rest to the bowl.

Put the oil, lime juice, miso, tahini, curry paste, ginger, and garlic in a small bowl. Whisk until thoroughly blended. Add the dressing to the vegetable mixture and toss with a silicone spatula until evenly distributed. Add the avocado and toss very gently, taking care to avoid mashing the avocado. Garnish with the reserved cilantro and serve at once.

Per serving: 566 calories, 19 g protein, 38 g fat (4 g sat), 42 g carbohydrates, 767 mg sodium, 162 mg calcium, 15 g fiber

TIP▶ Be sure to read the label when buying Thai curry paste, as most traditional brands contain dried shrimp.

This is an unusual application for romesco sauce, and an unorthodox combination of ingredients, but I think you'll be surprised how well they meld. Instead of the traditional method of serving the sauce over grilled vegetables, here the sauce almost becomes the base of the salad itself, a rich cloud of intoxicating flavors, punctuated by

grilled vegetable salad
WITH ROMESCO SAUCE

MAKES 8 SERVINGS

2 poblano chiles

2 ears white corn, shucked and silk removed

2 medium zucchini, cut lengthwise into thick strips

2 portobello mushrooms, stemmed

2 tablespoons extra-virgin olive oil

½ teaspoon sea salt

½ teaspoon freshly ground black pepper

1 red onion, finely diced

2 tablespoons freshly squeezed lime juice

½ cup chopped fresh cilantro leaves and tender stems, lightly packed

1 cup Romesco Sauce (page 30), plus more as needed

1 head red leaf lettuce or butter lettuce, torn into bite-sized pieces

Preheat the broiler. Line a baking sheet with foil.

Quarter the poblano chiles lengthwise and remove the stems, seed cluster, and membranes. Put the chiles on the prepared baking sheet and broil for 10 to 15 minutes, until the skins are evenly blackened. Immediately transfer the chiles to a small bowl and cover tightly with a pot lid, a plate, or aluminum foil. Let steam in the bowl until barely warm, about 15 minutes. Uncover and pour cold water into the bowl to loosen the skins. Remove and discard the skins. If the skins prove difficult to remove in spots, just leave them on and proceed. Cut the chiles into ½-inch squares.

the bits of charred vegetables floating in it. The first time I made this, I presented it as an appetizer, with small spoonfuls of the salad nestled in lettuce cups. The inner leaves of butter lettuce are perfect for this. Regardless of how you choose to serve this salad, it's a sure-fire crowd-pleaser.

Preheat a gas or charcoal grill (see tip) on high and put the corn on it. Turn the corn as needed to char the surface evenly, about 10 minutes. Don't worry if the corn appears to be badly burned in spots; the flavor imparted will be very agreeable when combined with the other ingredients. Wrap the charred corn in a sheet of foil and let steam in the residual heat until cool enough to handle. Unwrap and cut the kernels off the cobs into a large bowl.

Arrange the zucchini and mushrooms in a single layer on a baking sheet. Brush both sides of the vegetables with the oil and sprinkle with the salt and pepper. Transfer the vegetables to the grill and cook for 2 minutes. Turn them over and cook for 2 minutes longer. Remove from the grill and return them to the baking sheet. Let cool. Cut the zucchini and mushrooms into ½-inch dice.

Add the chiles, zucchini, mushrooms, onion, and lime juice to the corn and toss gently with a silicone spatula. Add ¼ cup of the cilantro and 1 cup of the sauce and toss until evenly distributed. Taste and add more sauce if desired.

Divide the lettuce among 4 salad plates, spreading it into a bed on each plate. Top with the grilled vegetable mixture, mounding it slightly. Garnish liberally with the remaining cilantro. Serve at once.

Per serving: 222 calories, 5 g protein, 17 g fat (2 g sat), 16 g carbohydrates, 216 mg sodium, 28 mg calcium, 4 g fiber

TIP▶ A grill will create the best flavor for the corn. However, if you don't have a grill, you can "grill" the corn by placing it on the flame of a gas stove or, as a last resort, under a broiler.

Many Japanese salads are served in small bowls, with an oil-free, brothy dressing like the one in this recipe. A packaged blend of different sea vegetables can be bought at Asian markets and many natural food stores. If the seaweed blend is

japanese SEAWEED SALAD

MAKES 8 SERVINGS

1 ounce seaweed blend

1 ounce dried shiitake mushrooms

3 cups water

2 ounces mung bean noodles
(optional)

1 Japanese cucumber, or 2 baby
cucumbers, peeled if desired
and thinly sliced on a diagonal

1 cup Kombu Dashi (page 18)

½ cup brown rice vinegar

¼ cup reduced-sodium tamari

¼ cup mirin

4 scallions, thinly sliced on a sharp
diagonal

Put the seaweed blend and mushrooms in a medium bowl. Add the water and let soak for 25 to 30 minutes. Drain the vegetables in a strainer set over another bowl, pressing down gently to extract the excess water. Transfer the vegetables to a large bowl.

Pour the soaking water into a small saucepan and bring to a boil over high heat. Remove from the heat and add the optional mung bean noodles, stirring to loosen them. Let stand for 3 minutes. Drain the noodles in the strainer (save the liquid for another use, if you like, as it will be flavorful and nutritious). Rinse the noodles under cold running water for about 30 seconds. Drain well and add to the bowl with the seaweed and mushrooms. Add the cucumber.

unavailable in your area, you can make this salad with only wakame, a sea vegetable that is very easy to find. Don't be fooled by what seems like a very small quantity of seaweed; it will swell to many times its size when reconstituted in water.

Put the dashi, vinegar, tamari, and mirin in a small bowl and stir. Pour over the vegetables and stir gently with a silicone spatula. Add the scallions and stir. Serve the salad in small bowls, with plenty of the brothy dressing.

Per serving: 60 calories, 2 g protein, 0 g fat (0 g sat), 10 g carbohydrates, 400 mg sodium, 43 mg calcium, 2 g fiber

Go for Extraordinary! The optional mung bean noodles, also known as *saifun*, or cellophane noodles, add body and textural interest to the salad, so they are highly recommended. Unlike other noodles, they are made from mung beans, not grains.

ARTICHOKE AND LENTIL salad

I much prefer fresh artichokes to canned or jarred, but quality brands can certainly help make a quick meal very easy. If you have cooked lentils on hand, you can make this salad lickety-split. All you'll need to do is pull a jar of artichokes from the pantry, dice a shallot, chop some herbs, and the rest can be done in a flash.

3 tablespoons extra-virgin olive oil

2 tablespoons freshly squeezed lemon juice

2 tablespoons sherry vinegar or additional lemon juice

1 teaspoon Dijon mustard

¼ teaspoon sea salt

¼ teaspoon freshly ground black pepper

1 tablespoon chopped fresh parsley

2 teaspoons chopped fresh thyme

3 cups cooked French lentils or other lentils, well drained

12 canned artichoke hearts, rinsed, patted dry, and cut in half lengthwise

⅓ cup minced shallots

Put the oil, lemon juice, vinegar, mustard, salt, and pepper in a medium bowl and whisk until emulsified. Add the parsley and thyme and whisk until incorporated. Add the lentils, artichokes, and shallots and toss until well combined. Serve at once.

Per serving: 328 calories, 16 g protein, 11 g fat (2 g sat), 42 g carbohydrates, 682 mg sodium, 68 mg calcium, 14 g fiber

TIP▶ This salad can be made up to two days in advance and brought to room temperature before serving or, if you're in a hurry, served cold.

Rajma Dal Bourguignon, page 96

Black Rice Cakes with Avocados and Braised Lotus Roots, page 106

Artichokes and Fennel with Preserved Lemon and Saffron, *page 110*

Mediterranean Eggplant Stack, page 122

When I was in India, I had an extraordinary dish made with dried cauliflower. It was so memorable that I've wanted to replicate the effect ever since. Although dried Indian cauliflower isn't available in the United States, roasted cauliflower provides an impressively similar flavor profile. When the cauliflower is combined with roasted beets, the result is nothing short of sublime.

ROASTED
cauliflower and beet salad

MAKES 8 SERVINGS

1 head cauliflower

7 small beets, scrubbed and quartered lengthwise

1 red onion, finely diced

½ cup extra-virgin olive oil

1½ tablespoons chopped fresh thyme

½ teaspoon sea salt

½ teaspoon freshly ground black pepper

3 tablespoons aged balsamic vinegar or Poor Man's Aged Balsamic Vinegar (page 10)

1 tablespoon chopped fresh parsley

Preheat the oven to 375 degrees F. Line a baking sheet with parchment paper.

Cut the cauliflower into large florets, about three times a standard bite-sized piece, and keep the stems as long as possible. The pieces will shrink considerably as they roast, so don't make them too small. Put the cauliflower, beets, onion, oil, ½ tablespoon of the thyme, and the salt and pepper in a bowl. Toss well to thoroughly coat the cauliflower and beets. Spread the mixture evenly on the prepared baking sheet. Roast in the oven for 35 to 40 minutes, until lightly browned, stirring every 10 minutes.

Slide the contents of the baking sheet, including any browned bits and accumulated juices, into a large bowl. Add the remaining thyme and the vinegar and parsley. Toss thoroughly, and then let cool. Serve at room temperature in small bowls.

Per serving: 110 calories, 2 g protein, 7 g fat (1 g sat), 10 g carbohydrates, 203 mg sodium, 25 mg calcium, 3 g fiber

When I buy baby spinach, I like to go through and pick out the tiniest, most pristine leaves to use in a salad. The rest I use for cooking, as in recipes like Sautéed Spinach with Roasted Garlic and Aleppo Pepper (page 121). The other star protagonist of this dish is fuyu persimmon. Unlike its American cousin, the Japanese fuyu is firm when ripe, and rather than being astringent, it's mildly sweet, with a pleasant texture that works very well in a salad. This is a dish guaranteed to impress your guests.

baby spinach salad
WITH BRAISED ONIONS AND FUYU PERSIMMONS

MAKES 4 SERVINGS

1 large red onion

3 tablespoons extra-virgin olive oil

1 bay leaf

½ teaspoon sea salt

¼ teaspoon freshly ground black pepper

¼ cup aged balsamic vinegar or Poor Man's Aged Balsamic Vinegar (page 10)

1 teaspoon Dutch-processed cocoa

1 tablespoon freshly squeezed lemon juice

1 teaspoon Dijon mustard

2 fuyu persimmons

1 pound baby spinach, washed and spun dry

1 cup pecans, lightly toasted

Quarter the onion lengthwise, and then cut it crosswise into ¼-inch slices. Heat the oil in a medium saucepan over medium heat until fragrant, about 30 seconds. Add the onion and cook, stirring frequently, until softened, about 2 minutes. Add the bay leaf, salt, and pepper and cook, stirring constantly, for 1 minute. Add 3 tablespoons of the vinegar and the cocoa and stir well. Decrease the heat to low, cover, and cook for 5 minutes. Remove from the heat and let cool completely. Remove and discard the bay leaf. Put the mixture in a strainer and drain the braising juices into a medium bowl. Set the onion aside.

Add the remaining 1 tablespoon of vinegar and the lemon juice and mustard to the braising juices and whisk until well combined.

Peel the persimmons. Cut them into wedges about ¼ inch thick at the wide end and remove any seeds. Put the persimmons, spinach, and onion in a large bowl. Add the lemon juice mixture and toss until evenly distributed. Add the pecans and toss again. Divide the salad among 4 plates and serve at once.

Per serving: 356 calories, 5 g protein, 28 g fat (3 g sat), 26 g carbohydrates, 361 mg sodium, 83 mg calcium, 8 g fiber

CHAPTER 8

beans and lentils

I grew up in Mexico, the land of corn and beans. For me, the smell of beans cooking is an emotional trigger that takes me back to the best moments of my childhood. In meat-centric cultures, beans and lentils are generally regarded as side dishes, the same way vegetables are, and little attention is given to preparing them. But in most agrarian cultures, beans and lentils play a central role in meals, for both nutrition and enjoyment. For example, in Indian cuisine they are, along with rice and vegetables, primary components of every meal, and their preparation is just as important as that of the most sophisticated meat-based dish. Millions of people not only subsist but thrive on a diet consisting of beans or lentils and rice almost exclusively. I think that should put to rest the recurring question posed to vegans and vegetarians about their sources of protein.

The word *arabesque* refers to a flight of fancy in music, so why not also apply it to food? To give this dish an Arabic flavor, I used baharat, a spice mixture used primarily in the cuisine of the Persian Gulf, Aleppo pepper, pomegranate molasses, and saffron. The fresh herbs gratuitously added at the end help ignite a multilayered riot of flavor.

ARABESQUE garbanzo beans

¼ cup extra-virgin olive oil

2 large yellow onions, cut into ½-inch dice

9 very young zucchini, cut into ½-inch dice

3 Roasted Red Peppers (page 14), cut into ½-inch dice

12 cloves Roasted Garlic (page 12), mashed into a paste

5 cups cooked garbanzo beans, with liquid

1 tablespoon baharat or ras el hanout

1 tablespoon Aleppo pepper, or ½ teaspoon red chile powder

1 tablespoon pomegranate molasses or freshly squeezed lemon juice

¼ teaspoon sea salt, plus more as needed

Large pinch saffron (optional)

½ cup chopped fresh cilantro, lightly packed

½ cup chopped fresh mint, lightly packed

Heat the oil in a large saucepan over medium-high heat until fragrant, about 30 seconds. Add the onions and cook, stirring frequently, until they have softened and are just beginning to brown, 4 to 5 minutes. Add the zucchini and cook, stirring often, for 5 minutes. Add the roasted red peppers and garlic and stir well to combine. Add the garbanzo beans and their liquid and the baharat, Aleppo pepper, pomegranate molasses, salt, and optional saffron. Cook, stirring frequently, until the liquid has been absorbed and the mixture is nearly dry, about 10 minutes. Remove from the heat and stir in the cilantro and mint. Serve at once, in bowls or on plates.

Per serving: 294 calories, 10 g protein, 9 g fat (1 g sat), 47 g carbohydrates, 622 mg sodium, 204 mg calcium, 10 g fiber

Go for Extraordinary! A Middle Eastern staple made by reducing pure pomegranate juice to a thick syrup, pomegranate molasses imparts a pleasant, tangy fruit note. I like using it with dishes that are not Middle Eastern in origin, just to stretch the envelope a little. Many supermarkets now carry it in their international sections.

This was an experiment gone terribly right. The garbanzo beans turned a gorgeous amethyst color, and although combining them with beets is unorthodox—especially with the spices and preserved lemon—I think you'll find the flavors meld like lovers. Like many Mediterranean dishes, this one works equally well hot, room temperature, or cold.

garbanzos WITH BEETS

See photo facing page 55.

MAKES 4 SERVINGS

2 tablespoons extra-virgin olive oil

1 large yellow or red onion, cut into ½-inch dice

2 red beets, cut into ½-inch dice

4 cloves garlic, minced

1 unsalted vegetable bouillon cube

1 teaspoon ras' el hanout or curry powder

½ teaspoon sea salt

¼ teaspoon freshly ground black pepper

3 cups cooked garbanzo beans, liquid reserved separately

¼ preserved lemon (see page 16), **rind only, cut into ¼-inch dice** (optional)

¼ cup chopped fresh mint, lightly packed

Heat the oil in a large saucepan over medium-high heat until fragrant, about 30 seconds. Add the onion and cook, stirring frequently, until softened, about 2 minutes. Add the beets and garlic and cook, stirring often, for 5 minutes. Add the bouillon cube, ras el hanout, salt, and pepper and stir well. If the mixture is very dry, add 1 to 2 tablespoons of water. Cover and cook for 10 minutes, stirring often and occasionally adding 1 tablespoon of water as needed to keep the mixture from sticking.

Add the beans and optional preserved lemon and stir well. If the mixture is very dry, stir in about ¼ cup of the bean cooking liquid to keep the mixture moist and prevent sticking. Cover and cook for 5 minutes, stirring frequently and adding more bean cooking liquid as needed. When the beets are tender, remove from the heat and stir in the mint. Serve at once.

Per serving: 333 calories, 10 g protein, 11 g fat (2 g sat), 52 g carbohydrates, 873 mg sodium, 140 mg calcium, 112 g fiber

TIP▶ If you prefer, you can use canned no-salt-added garbanzo beans. Drain and rinse them before adding, and substitute water for the cooking liquid.

HOGLESS hoppin' john

Every culture has its traditional dish served on New Year's Day that's intended to bring luck in the coming year. In the southern United States, dishes with black-eyed peas are believed to help start the year off right, and one of the most popular is called hoppin' john, traditionally made with smoked ham hocks. In my version, far better for the health of both humans and animals, smoked salt and smoked paprika provide the smokehouse touch.

1 pound dried black-eyed peas, picked over, rinsed, and soaked in water for 8 to 12 hours

5 tablespoons extra-virgin olive oil

2 yellow or red onions, diced

3 stalks celery, diced

2 carrots, scrubbed and diced

1 green bell pepper, diced

2 serrano or jalapeño chiles, finely diced

7 cloves garlic, minced

4 cups water

2 unsalted vegetable bouillon cubes

½ teaspoon smoked salt or sea salt

½ teaspoon smoked paprika

9 leaves collard greens, center ribs removed, stacked and cut into ½-inch squares

2 cups cooked rice (optional)

2 ripe tomatoes, cut into bite-sized chunks

10 scallions, sliced

Drain the black-eyed peas and put them in a large saucepan. Cover with water by 4 inches and bring to a boil over high heat. Decrease the heat to medium. Skim off any foam that rises and discard. Once the foaming ceases, add 2 tablespoons of the oil. Simmer until the peas are tender, about 1½ hours.

Put the remaining 3 tablespoons of oil in a large saucepan over medium-high heat. Add the onions, celery, carrots, bell pepper, chiles, and garlic and stir well. Cook, stirring frequently, until the vegetables are just beginning to stick, about 5 minutes. Add the water, bouillon cubes, salt, and paprika and bring to a boil. Add the collard greens and stir. Decrease the heat to medium-low and simmer until the vegetables are just tender, about 20 minutes. Drain the black-eyed peas and add them to the vegetables. Simmer until the vegetables are very tender and the mixture has thickened into a stew, about 20 minutes.

For each serving, put a large spoonful of the optional rice in the center of a large soup bowl. Ladle the black-eyed pea mixture over the rice. Garnish with the tomatoes and scallions or pass them at the table. Serve at once.

Per serving: 650 calories, 31 g protein, 21 g fat (4 g sat), 84 g carbohydrates, 497 mg sodium, 230 mg calcium, 23 g fiber

Go for Extraordinary! I use smoked salt rarely, but it keeps indefinitely and is an ideal way to add a smoky flavor to dishes like this one that warrant it.

masoor dal
WITH KABOCHA SQUASH

MAKES 4 SERVINGS

Known as *masoor dal* in India, the orange-red lentils used in this dish turn yellow as they cook. They make a striking appearance when combined with deep orange kabocha squash. This is essentially a one-dish meal, which you can reheat for lunch or a snack if you like. Traditionally, dal is served either in a small bowl or over rice. Your call.

1 cup masoor dal or split red lentils, picked over, rinsed, and drained

12 cups water, as needed

2 tablespoons extra-virgin olive oil

1 large yellow or red onion, finely diced

7 cloves garlic, minced

5 cups peeled and diced kabocha or butternut squash

1 tablespoon curry powder

2 unsalted vegetable bouillon cubes

½ teaspoon sea salt, plus more as needed

¼ teaspoon hot red chile powder, plus more as needed

½ cup chopped fresh cilantro, lightly packed

Put the dal in a medium saucepan with 4 cups of the water. Bring to a boil over high heat. Decrease the heat to medium and simmer until the lentils are very tender and have nearly dissolved, about 45 minutes.

Meanwhile, heat the oil in a large soup pot over medium-high heat until fragrant, about 30 seconds. Add the onion and cook, stirring frequently, until it begins to soften, about 2 minutes. Add the garlic and cook, stirring constantly, for 1 minute. Add the squash and cook, stirring frequently, for 2 minutes. Add the curry powder and mix well. Add 6 cups of the water and the bouillon cubes, salt, and chile powder and bring to a boil.

Decrease the heat to medium and cook, stirring occasionally, until all the vegetables are tender, about 25 minutes. Add more of the water if needed to prevent sticking.

When the dal is tender, add it to the pot of vegetables and stir well. Cook, stirring frequently, until the mixture thickens, about 5 minutes. Taste and add more salt and chile powder if desired. Simmer for 5 minutes longer to allow the flavors to meld. Remove from the heat and stir in the cilantro. Serve at once.

Per serving: 385 calories, 17 g protein, 9 g fat (2 g sat), 60 g carbohydrates, 394 mg sodium, 190 mg calcium, 12 g fiber

TIP▶ Masoor dal is available at Indian markets and in the international section of well-stocked supermarkets. Many natural food stores also carry it under the name "red lentils."

No doubt about it, this recipe is a labor of love. The magic behind the classic French dish boeuf bourguignon is the reduction of red wine with herbs and vegetables. In this cleaner, kinder version, an Indian red bean called *rajma dal*

RAJMA DAL **bourguignon**

See photo facing page 86.   MAKES 6 SERVINGS

1 pound rajma dal or other red beans, picked over, rinsed, and soaked in water for 8 to 12 hours

12 sprigs parsley

12 sprigs thyme

4 tablespoons extra-virgin olive oil

2 yellow onions, finely diced

2 carrots, scrubbed and finely diced

2 stalks celery, finely diced

2 cloves garlic, minced

1¼ teaspoons sea salt, plus more as needed

¼ teaspoon freshly ground black pepper, plus more as needed

3 tablespoons cognac (optional)

1½ cups no-salt-added tomato purée

2 bay leaves

1 bottle red wine, preferably burgundy

12 ounces mushrooms, washed and quartered lengthwise

24 frozen pearl onions

1 tablespoon coconut oil

1 tablespoon evaporated cane juice crystals

3 slices gluten-free sourdough bread

2 tablespoons chopped fresh parsley

Put the beans in a large saucepan and cover with water by 4 inches. Bring to a boil over high heat. Decrease the heat to medium and simmer until the beans are tender, about 2 hours. If you need to add more water to keep the beans well covered, add boiling water.

While the beans are cooking, tie the parsley and thyme sprigs into a bundle with kitchen twine. Heat 2 tablespoons of the oil in a large saucepan over high heat until fragrant, about 30 seconds. Add the yellow onions, carrots, celery, garlic, ¼ teaspoon of the salt, and the pepper and stir well. Decrease the heat to medium and cook, stirring frequently, until the vegetables are just beginning to stick, about 5 minutes. Add the optional cognac and stand back to save your facial hair from the flames. Stir in the tomato purée and bring to a boil over medium-high heat. Decrease the heat to medium. Add the herb bundle along with the bay leaves. Cook, stirring occasionally, until the vegetables are very tender, about 1 hour. Remove and discard the herb bundle and bay leaves.

supplants the beef and greatly improves the flavor of the dish. Except for the animal products, all of the traditional components remain, right down to the parsley-dipped heart-shaped toasts.

While the vegetables are cooking, pour the wine into a medium saucepan and bring to a boil over high heat. Decrease the heat to medium-low and simmer until the wine has reduced to about ½ cup, 20 to 30 minutes. Remove from the heat and add to the vegetables, scraping the saucepan with a silicone spatula to get every last bit.

When the beans are tender, add the remaining teaspoon of salt and continue cooking for 5 minutes longer. Add the beans and their cooking liquid to the vegetables. Cook, stirring often, until the liquid is reduced and the mixture has thickened into a stew, 10 to 20 minutes.

Heat 1 tablespoon of the oil in a skillet and heat over medium-high heat until fragrant, about 30 seconds. Add the mushrooms and a pinch of salt and pepper, and cook, shaking the skillet occasionally to toss and turn the mushrooms, until lightly browned and tender, about 5 minutes. Set aside.

Put the pearl onions in a saucepan just large enough to accommodate them in a single layer and add enough water to cover them about halfway. Add the coconut oil, evaporated cane juice crystals, and a pinch of salt and pepper, and bring to a boil over high heat. Cook, shaking the pan occasionally, until the water has evaporated, about 15 minutes. Shake the pan constantly as the sugars begin to caramelize and coat the onions. As soon as the onions are evenly browned and sticky, remove the pan from the heat and set aside.

To make the toast garnishes, preheat the oven to 400 degrees F. Cut the bread slices in half. Trim each piece into a heart shape or cut with a heart-shaped cookie cutter. Brush the hearts with 1 tablespoon of the oil and put them on a baking sheet. Bake for about 7 minutes, until lightly browned. Let cool.

When the bean mixture is ready, stir in the mushrooms and pearl onions. Ladle into shallow soup bowls. Dip the points of the heart toasts into the sauce, then into the parsley, and set on the rims of the bowls. Garnish with the remaining parsley and serve at once.

Per serving: 618 calories, 29 g protein, 13 g fat (4 g sat), 79 g carbohydrates, 775 mg sodium, 166 mg calcium, 27 g fiber

The beauty and flexibility of lentils is greatly overlooked. I had never thought of pairing them with fennel, for example, until thirty years into my career in food. Even when the idea came, I wasn't certain it would work, but the result was fairly spectacular. Fennel is a soothing vegetable, and it's beneficial for digestion. It also has an unusual way of both standing out and blending in nicely. I named this dish after a fine gentleman I was serving at the time.

RUDOLF'S lentils

MAKES 8 SERVINGS

¼ cup extra-virgin olive oil

1 cup finely diced shallots

4 cups diced fennel

1 pound French lentils, picked over, rinsed, and drained

6 cups water

2 unsalted vegetable bouillon cubes

1 bay leaf

1 teaspoon sea salt, plus more as needed

2 tablespoons Pernod (optional)

Snipped chives or chopped fresh parsley, for garnish

Heat the oil in a large soup pot over medium-high heat until fragrant, about 30 seconds. Add the shallots and cook, stirring constantly, until they have softened, about 3 minutes. Don't let them brown. Add the fennel and stir to combine. Cook, stirring frequently, until the fennel begins to soften and color lightly, about 5 minutes. Add the lentils and stir well. Add the water, bouillon cubes, and bay leaf. Increase the heat to high and bring to a boil. Decrease the heat to medium-low, cover, and cook until the lentils are very tender, about 45 minutes.

Remove and discard the bay leaf. Stir in the salt and cook for 5 minutes longer. Add the Pernod, if using, and stir for about 30 seconds. Serve the lentils in small bowls, garnished with the chives.

Per serving: 247 calories, 15 g protein, 8 g fat (2 g sat), 20 g carbohydrates, 346 mg sodium, 15 mg calcium, 18 g fiber

For many people who decide to go vegan, especially all at once, the change is radical enough without also switching from white flour bread and pasta to eating whole grains. But to enjoy the full health benefits of leaving animal products behind, it's a good idea to try cutting back on refined food, especially refined grains and sugar. Happily, gluten-free brown rice pasta has arrived on the scene, with a taste and texture very close to the Italian pasta well-loved the world over. Also, a number of whole grains, like black rice and red rice, and "pseudograins," such as amaranth, buckwheat, quinoa, and wild rice, that were once considered exotic by many, are now commonplace.

pasta and grains

In modern Western cuisine, grains have had a rather pedestrian function as a kind of "filler," a neutral couch on which other foods with real flavor would rest. In this limited role, it was ideal for them to be as bland and soft-textured as possible. But in a cuisine built on healthful principles, whole grains with unique properties, chewier textures, and assertive flavors become major players in their own right. The notion that grains are merely included to provide a feeling of fullness has been replaced with the sheer pleasure of eating them in their robust natural form and wonderful variety. This is a boon to any cook, especially a cook looking to create an extraordinary eating experience.

A lady from Bari, on the west coast of Italy, gave me this idea as I was standing in line at an Italian market. It's a very simple but vibrant affair, with the potent flavors of the Mezzogiorno, the middle Italian peninsula: garlic, chile, olive oil, and bitter greens. The secret is not to overcook the greens, so you can enjoy a very fresh taste and texture. I recommend using Aleppo pepper because it adds a delicious dimension of exotic flavor, but red chile flakes are also very good here.

ziti WITH BROCCOLI RABE AND CANNELLINI BEANS

MAKES 4 SERVINGS

1 large bunch broccoli rabe (about 1½ pounds)

1 tablespoon sea salt (optional)

¼ cup plus 2 tablespoons extra-virgin olive oil

9 large cloves garlic, thinly sliced

1 tablespoon Aleppo pepper, or 1 teaspoon crushed red pepper flakes

½ teaspoon sea salt

Freshly ground black pepper (optional)

2 cups cooked cannellini beans, or 1 can (25 ounces) no-salt-added cannellini beans, drained and rinsed

8 ounces brown rice ziti or penne

Wash the broccoli rabe and shake off the excess water. Pinch the florets off the stems and put them in a small bowl. Cut the leafy portions, including the stems, into ½-inch-thick slices, and then coarsely chop them just to shorten any long strips.

Fill a large pot with water. Add the optional tablespoon of salt and bring to a boil over high heat. Add the florets and stir once. Add the leaves and stems and stir again. Cook for 1 minute, then drain the broccoli rabe in a colander set over a large bowl to catch the cooking liquid. Immediately rinse the broccoli rabe under cold running water and leave to drain in the colander. Return the hot cooking liquid to the pot, cover, and bring to a boil over high heat.

While the water is reheating, put ¼ cup of the oil and the garlic in a large, heavy skillet over medium-high heat. Shake the skillet back and forth to keep the garlic moving. As soon as the garlic begins to color lightly, add the Aleppo pepper and ½ teaspoon salt. Continue shaking the pan until the garlic has turned light tan, about 2 minutes. Immediately add the broccoli rabe and stir well. Add the beans and heat until warmed through, 2 to 3 minutes. Remove from the heat.

When the water is boiling again, add the ziti and stir well to prevent sticking. Cook until the ziti is tender but firm, about 7 minutes. Drain, reserving a little of the cooking liquid, and return the ziti to the pot. Stir in the remaining 2 tablespoons of oil, shaking the pot to coat the ziti well. Add the broccoli rabe mixture and heat through, shaking the pan to combine well. Serve at once, in shallow soup bowls.

Per serving: 466 calories, 18 g protein, 16 g fat (2 g sat), 65 g carbohydrates, 98 mg sodium, 345 mg calcium, 12 g fiber

spaghetti A-O-P

There are several sauces that can be made in the time it takes for the water to boil and cook the pasta, but this one is by far the most thrilling. It's spicy and pungent, but it allows the pasta to hold its own at center stage. It's perfect, really. "A-O-P" stands for "*aglio-olio-peperoncino*," Italian for "garlic, oil, and chile pepper," an all-time favorite of mine. You can also use this sauce to brush on grilled slices of bread, with or without the chile.

3 dried red chiles, stems removed

1 tablespoon sea salt (optional)

½ cup plus 2 tablespoons extra-virgin olive oil

⅓ cup chopped fresh Italian parsley, lightly packed

7 cloves garlic, coarsely chopped

½ teaspoon sea salt

1 pound brown rice spaghetti or other spaghetti

Put the chiles in a small bowl or jar and cover with boiling water. Set aside to soak until softened, 8 to 10 minutes.

Fill a large pot with water. Add the optional tablespoon of salt and 2 tablespoons of the oil. Bring to a boil over high heat.

Remove the chiles from the water, pat dry with a towel, and chop coarsely with a sharp knife. Add the parsley and garlic and chop finely. Scrape the mixture into a small bowl and add the remaining ½ cup of oil and the ½ teaspoon of salt. Stir well.

When the water is boiling, add the spaghetti and stir well to prevent sticking. Cook until the spaghetti is tender but firm. Drain and return to the pot. Stir in the chile mixture and shake the pot to coat the spaghetti. Serve at once, in shallow soup bowls.

Per serving: 659 calories, 9 g protein, 30 g fat (4 g sat), 92 g carbohydrates, 338 mg sodium, 12 mg calcium, 3 g fiber

TIP▶ There will be a little sauce left in the pot. To get it out, twirl some spaghetti on a fork and use that to mop it up.

Soba noodles made with 100 percent buckwheat flour are getting hard to find these days, but they're worth hunting around for. They're truly whole grain, with an earthy flavor unmatched in the gluten-free noodle kingdom. I've paired them here with Japanese elements because I think they belong with the flavors of their origin. That's just me, though; feel free to use them any way that inspires you.

buckwheat soba
WITH BEAN SPROUTS

MAKES 2 SERVINGS

3 ounces dried shiitake mushrooms

12 ounces buckwheat soba noodles

3 tablespoons reduced-sodium tamari

2 tablespoons Kombu Dashi (page 18)

2 tablespoons mirin

1 tablespoon mellow white miso

1 teaspoon sriracha sauce

8 ounces mung bean sprouts

1 tablespoon flax oil

1 teaspoon toasted sesame oil

10 scallions, thinly sliced

1 tablespoon sesame seeds

Carefully break off and discard any stems from the mushrooms. Put the caps in a small bowl and cover with warm water. Let soak until reconstituted, about 20 minutes. Remove the mushrooms from the water, slice thinly, and put them on a plate.

Pour the mushroom soaking liquid through a towel into a medium saucepan, and add enough fresh water to come within 1½ inches from the rim of the pan. Bring to a boil over high heat and add the noodles. Stir to prevent the noodles from sticking and cook until tender but not mushy, about 5 minutes.

While the noodles are cooking, put the tamari, dashi, mirin, miso, and sriracha sauce in a small bowl and stir until well combined. As soon as the noodles are done, add the bean sprouts and mushrooms and stir for 10 seconds. Drain in a colander and immediately return to the saucepan. Add the flax oil and sesame oil and shake the saucepan to coat the noodles. Add the tamari mixture and warm through over medium-low heat. Do not boil. Remove from the heat and stir in the scallions. Divide between two bowls. Garnish with the sesame seeds and serve at once.

Per serving: 879 calories, 33 g protein, 14 g fat (1 g sat), 153 g carbohydrates, 1,964 mg sodium, 113 mg calcium, 12 g fiber

polenta WITH PEPPERS

When I was a college student living in Ticino, the Italian part of Switzerland, I came across polenta for the first time. It's a regional dish in both Ticino and Lombardy (on the Italian side), where the residents are extremely particular about the way their polenta is prepared. It must be cooked very slowly and stirred constantly in order to get a light, creamy, slightly grainy texture. Some restaurants in the area have a special machine set up in the front window, where passersby can see a large pot of polenta cooking. The machine has an automatic mechanism that stirs the polenta nonstop. For home cooking, a heavy saucepan is very helpful in preventing the polenta from sticking and burning.

3 cups water

1 unsalted vegetable bouillon cube

½ teaspoon sea salt

1 cup polenta or yellow corn grits

2 tablespoons extra-virgin olive oil

6 cups Peperonata (page 32)

1 tablespoon chopped fresh parsley

Put the water, bouillon cube, and salt in a medium saucepan and bring to a boil over high heat. Slowly add the polenta, whisking vigorously to prevent lumps. When the mixture returns to a boil, decrease the heat to low, cover, and cook, stirring frequently, for 30 minutes. Stir in the oil, cover, and keep warm on the lowest setting while heating the Peperonata.

Heat the Peperonata in a medium saucepan over medium-high heat until bubbling. Divide the polenta among four plates and drape 1 cup of the Peperonata across the top of each serving. Garnish with the parsley and serve at once, passing the remaining Peperonata at the table.

Per serving: 315 calories, 7 g protein, 17 g fat (4 g sat), 40 g carbohydrates, 937 mg sodium, 147 mg calcium, 10 g fiber

VARIATION▶ Instead of Peperonata, serve the polenta with Wild Mushroom Ragoût (page 113).

carrot-cardamom
RICE WITH SAFFRON

Although white rice has gotten a bit of a bum health rap, I make a rare exception for basmati rice, as there truly is no good substitute. Plus, the smell of basmati rice as it's cooking is nothing short of heavenly.

1 cup basmati rice

1 cup carrot juice

½ cup water

1 tablespoon extra-virgin coconut oil

4 green cardamom pods, lightly crushed

½ teaspoon sea salt

Pinch saffron

Wash the rice in a bowl with water. This must be done very gently to avoid breaking the grains. Change the water frequently, until it runs clear. Drain well.

Put the rice in a small saucepan. Add the carrot juice, water, oil, cardamom, salt, and saffron. Bring to a boil over high heat. Decrease the heat to low, cover, and cook for 12 minutes. Remove from the heat and fluff the grains very gently with a silicone spatula. Serve at once.

Per serving: 210 calories, 3 g protein, 4 g fat (3 g sat), 37 g carbohydrates, 323 mg sodium, 10 mg calcium, 1 g fiber

Go for Extraordinary!
Make sure you buy true basmati rice. Look for it at an Indian grocery store, if possible, and ask for Dehraduni basmati rice. This is not just a starch to bulk up your meal; this is a delicious partner to virtually any vegetable dish, especially those with a juicy sauce. Unlike polished white rice, basmati is hand processed and retains a little of the bran (look at it with a magnifying glass and you'll see). The grains fluff lengthwise into elegant, long, fragrant gems. The smell of true basmati cooking is downright intoxicating. Once you've had the real thing, impostors will be obvious to you on sight (and smell).

There are thousands of varieties of quinoa in the Andes mountains, but so far in most markets only three varieties are available—white, red, and black. Some fair trade brands offer a mixture of all three in one package, but the black by itself is often hard to find. I prefer black quinoa for this dish because its texture is the firmest of the three varieties, although red quinoa is a close second choice.

black quinoa WITH CHAYOTES

MAKES 4 SERVINGS

1 cup black or red quinoa

1 unsalted vegetable bouillon cube

1 teaspoon sea salt

2½ cups water

2 tablespoons extra-virgin olive oil

1 large onion, finely diced

1 stalk celery, finely diced

1 leek, green part only, finely diced

4 cloves garlic, minced

2 chayotes, peeled, pitted, and cut into ½-inch dice

Zest of 1 tangelo or orange

Juice of 1 tangelo or orange

¼ teaspoon freshly ground black pepper

1 cup chopped fresh parsley, lightly packed

Put the quinoa, bouillon cube, and ½ teaspoon of the salt in a medium saucepan. Add the water and bring to a boil over high heat. Decrease the heat to low, cover, and cook until all the liquid is absorbed, about 25 minutes. Remove from the heat and set aside.

Heat the oil in a large, heavy saucepan over medium-low heat until fragrant, about 30 seconds, swirling to spread the oil evenly. Add the onion, celery, leek, and garlic and stir well. Spread the mixture out in an even layer. Decrease the heat to low, cover, and cook until tender, about 15 minutes. Check occasionally and add 1 tablespoon of water if needed to prevent the vegetables from sticking.

Increase the heat to medium-high and add the chayotes, stirring until the mixture is almost dry. Add the tangelo juice, the remaining ½ teaspoon of salt, and the pepper, stirring well. Decrease the heat to low, cover, and cook for 10 minutes. Check occasionally and add 1 to 2 tablespoons of water if needed to prevent sticking.

Add the quinoa and stir well. If the mixture is very dry, add 2 to 3 tablespoons of water and stir again. Cover and cook until all the liquid is absorbed and the chayotes are tender, about 5 minutes. Remove from the heat and stir in the tangelo zest and parsley. Stir gently but thoroughly. Serve at once.

Per serving: 308 calories, 8 g protein, 11 g fat (2 g sat), 47 g carbohydrates, 642 mg sodium, 98 mg calcium, 8 g fiber

Long ago, black rice was the sole property of the Chinese emperor. Hence, it was "forbidden" rice to everyone else. But he's gone now, along with his descendants, so everyone can enjoy the pleasure and health benefits of this unusual whole grain. It's actually not black but a very dark purple, due to a high concentration of anthocyanins, a potent class of antioxidants also found in blueberries and blackberries. As a cook, I'm more interested in the rice's dramatic appearance on the plate and its dense, unusual flavor.

black rice cakes
WITH AVOCADOS AND BRAISED LOTUS ROOTS

See photo between pages 86 and 87.   MAKES 4 SERVINGS

2¾ cups water, plus more as needed

1 cup forbidden rice

½ teaspoon sea salt

24 slices dried or fresh lotus root, preferably 1½ inches in diameter

¼ cup reduced-sodium tamari

¼ cup mirin

1 teaspoon toasted sesame oil

2 tablespoons sesame seeds

1 sheet nori

4 avocados

4 scallions, very thinly sliced on a sharp diagonal

2 teaspoons black sesame seeds

Put 1¾ cups of the water, the rice, and ¼ teaspoon of the salt in a small saucepan. Bring to a boil over high heat. Decrease the heat to low, cover, and cook for 35 minutes. Remove from the heat and fluff the rice with a silicone spatula. Cover and set aside.

If using dried lotus root, reconstitute it in water to cover by 1 inch for 20 minutes before proceeding. Put the lotus root, tamari, mirin, sesame oil, and remaining cup of water in a small saucepan. Bring to a boil over high heat. Decrease the heat to medium-low and cook until the lotus root is tender and the liquid has reduced to a thin sauce, about 20 minutes. The sauce should have the consistency of warm maple syrup. If the liquid reduces too quickly and the lotus root is still tough, add about ¼ cup of additional water and continue cooking until the lotus root is tender, 5 to 10 minutes longer. Remove from the heat, cover, and set aside.

Put the sesame seeds in a small skillet over medium-high heat. Toast them, shaking the skillet constantly, until light brown and aromatic, about 4 minutes. Pour the

seeds into a mortar, preferably a Japanese suribachi, and add the remaining ¼ teaspoon salt. Grind the seeds coarsely, leaving a few intact.

Preheat the oven to 250 degrees F.

Toast the nori over an open flame until it turns green and shrivels slightly. Alternatively, the nori can be toasted in a toaster oven, but keep a close eye on it so it doesn't burn. Break the nori into pieces in a small bowl, and then crumble it finely.

Pack the rice into a 3½-inch ring mold (see tip) to form a cylinder about 1¼ inches tall. Remove from the mold and transfer to a baking sheet. Repeat to form 3 more cakes, and then put all of the cakes in the oven to keep warm.

Cut the avocados in half lengthwise and remove the pits. Cut 3 equal slices across the center of the concave area where the pit was, and then use a large spoon to scoop out the flesh. You should have 24 arc-shaped slices. Reserve the other pieces for another use.

Select four medium-sized plates and put a rice cake in the center of each plate using a thin, wide spatula. Arrange 6 avocado slices on top of each cake, overlapping the slices to form a continuous circle right above the edge of the cake. Place 6 slices of the lotus root around each cake, spacing them evenly. Drizzle a thin stream of the sauce in a circle across the middle of each slice. Garnish with a very light sprinkling of the nori all around, followed by the scallions, the ground sesame seeds, and then the black sesame seeds. Serve at once.

Per serving: 549 calories, 13 g protein, 28 g fat (4 g sat), 70 g carbohydrates, 891 mg sodium, 118 mg calcium, 17 g fiber

TIP▶ A ring mold is a culinary tool designed to help form food into a uniform cylindrical shape for aesthetics. It's a simple stainless steel band, usually about 1½ to 2 inches wide. You can find various sizes at restaurant supply stores or online (see page 143). Alternatively, you can easily improvise a ring mold by using a can opener to remove both ends of an empty short tin can.

I like using as much of a plant as possible, especially in the same recipe. The most striking visual aspect of this dish is the deep purple-red color, but what inspires me is achieving the illusion of three distinctly different vegetables from one. There is the obvious beet, in large pieces; then the sliced stems, which most people have never eaten and might not be able to identify; and the green tops, which are easily confused with Swiss chard. The quinoa turns a bright amethyst color and is sweetened by the beets. A complex effect is achieved with the addition of just two vegetables and a little thyme.

quinoa WITH BEETS

MAKES 4 SERVINGS

2 large beets, with green tops

1 cup white quinoa

1 unsalted vegetable bouillon cube

½ teaspoon sea salt

2 cups water

2 tablespoons extra-virgin olive oil

1 large red onion, diced

2 cloves garlic, minced

¼ teaspoon freshly ground black pepper

2 teaspoons chopped fresh thyme

Scrub the beets and cut them into 1- to 1½-inch cubes. Wash the greens and stems thoroughly to remove any sandy grit or dirt. Remove the stems from the greens and cut them into ½-inch lengths. Chop the greens coarsely.

Put the quinoa, bouillon cube, and ¼ teaspoon of the salt in a small saucepan. Add the water and bring to a boil over high heat. Decrease the heat to low, cover, and cook for 20 minutes. Remove from the heat, fluff with a silicone spatula, replace the cover, and set aside.

Heat the oil in a large saucepan over medium-high heat until fragrant, about 30 seconds. Add the onion and cook, stirring frequently, until the onion softens, about 2 minutes. Add the beets and stir well. Decrease the heat to medium, cover, and cook, stirring frequently, for 10 minutes. Add the garlic, beet stems, remaining ¼ teaspoon of salt, and the pepper and stir well. Cover and cook, stirring frequently, for 10 minutes. If the vegetables begin to stick, add 1 tablespoon of water as needed. When the beets are tender, add the quinoa and thyme and stir well. Serve at once.

Per serving: 229 calories, 7 g protein, 4 g fat (1 g sat), 42 g carbohydrates, 432 mg sodium, 106 mg calcium, 8 g fiber

The diversity of vegetables available to us is staggering. What we see on the produce shelves at grocery stores is an infinitesimal fraction of the vast and wondrous array of wildly varied plant foods in existence. And each plant brings a unique blend of flavors, nutrients, and health benefits to the table.

Health experts tell us that we should eat as diverse an assortment of plant foods as possible to obtain all the nutrients various plants offer. Some also advise that we try to include all five tastes—sweet, sour, salty, bitter, and umami—the latter being a relatively new addition, translating roughly as "savory." In some traditions, hot (spicy) and pungent are included, both as tastes and as indicators of anti-inflammatory, antimicrobial, antiviral, and anticancer properties in a food. A variety of colors also ensures the inclusion of important health properties and other vital characteristics, not the least of which is pleasure—to the eye as much as to the palate.

vegetables

A cook's exalted role in the sacred dance of procuring, preparing, and supplying our bodies with the building blocks needed for optimum condition and functionality is to make food as enjoyable as possible. Remarkably, any of us can turn ordinary plants into extraordinary food.

I've paired artichokes and fennel in a number of different dishes over the years—soups, salads, relishes, fricassees, stews, tajines, and sandwiches—for the simple reason that they go together marvelously well. The two complement each other in the classic way that chocolate and vanilla do, but in a much more intimate mesh of flavor and texture.

artichokes and fennel
WITH PRESERVED LEMON AND SAFFRON

See photo between pages 86 and 87.   MAKES 4 SERVINGS

1 lemon

2 large globe artichokes

2 large fennel bulbs

½ large red onion

½ Preserved Lemon (page 16), with 1 tablespoon of the brine

3 tablespoons extra-virgin olive oil

1 cup dry white wine, preferably Pinot Grigio

Pinch of saffron

Sea salt

Freshly ground black pepper

1 teaspoon chopped fresh parsley

Cut the lemon in half and squeeze the juice into a medium bowl. Grasp an artichoke by the stem and snap off the dark green outer layer of leaves, one by one, until the lighter green leaves are exposed. Cut across the artichoke just above where the remaining leaves are attached. Cut away the tough, darker green exterior around the base of the artichoke, exposing the pale inner flesh. Rub all the exposed areas with the lemon to prevent discoloration. Cut the artichoke in half lengthwise, and then cut out the hairy choke from both halves. Cut each half into wedges, including the tender leaf portions, a little less than ½ inch at the wide end. As you cut, drop the wedges into the bowl of lemon juice, tossing them until they are evenly coated with the juice. Repeat with the second artichoke.

See how to prepare an artichoke.
youtu.be/bTvhOyDFVmQ

Cut the fennel in half lengthwise. Using a sharp paring knife, carve out most of the core, leaving just enough to hold the leaves together in one piece. Cut the fennel lengthwise into long sections about ¼ inch wide. Lay the onion on the cutting board cut-side down and cut it lengthwise into strips about ¼ inch wide. Scrape the pulp off the preserved lemon. Cut the rind into ¼-inch dice.

Put the olive oil in a large saucepan over medium-high heat. Add the onion and cook, stirring frequently, until it begins to soften and caramelize lightly, 4 to 5 minutes. Drain and add the artichokes and fennel. Cook, stirring frequently, until the artichokes and fennel are nearly dry and just beginning to color, 3 to 4 minutes. Add the preserved lemon, brine, and wine. Increase the heat to high and bring to a boil. Decrease the heat to medium-low, add the saffron, cover, and cook until the vegetables are tender, about 15 minutes. If a lot of liquid remains, increase the heat to high and cook, uncovered, shaking the saucepan back and forth, until the liquid thickens into a silky sauce. Season with salt and pepper to taste. Serve hot or at room temperature, garnished with the parsley.

Per serving: 200 calories, 4 g protein, 11 g fat (1 g sat), 19 g carbohydrates, 123 mg sodium, 100 mg calcium, 8 g fiber

curried
MUSHROOMS AND PEAS

MAKES 4 SERVINGS

The combination of mushrooms and peas is not a new one, yet simply by adding a little curry powder and freshly chopped cilantro, it becomes an exotic affair. Where once these vegetables may have been a side dish—mere window dressing to accompany an entree—here they play every bit as important a role as any other items on the plate, as I believe it should be.

2 tablespoons extra-virgin coconut oil

2 large onions, diced

1 pound button or cremini mushrooms, quartered lengthwise

2 tablespoons curry powder

1 unsalted vegetable bouillon cube

2 cups frozen peas

¼ teaspoon sea salt, plus more as needed

½ cup chopped fresh cilantro, lightly packed

1 tablespoon freshly squeezed lemon juice

Heat the oil in a large saucepan over high heat until fragrant, about 30 seconds. Add the onions and cook, stirring frequently, until the onions are soft, about 4 minutes. Add the mushrooms and stir gently. Decrease the heat to medium, cover, and cook for 2 minutes. Stir in the curry powder and bouillon cube. Add the peas and salt, stirring well. If the mixture is very dry, add ½ cup of water. Increase the heat to high and bring to a simmer. Decrease the heat to medium and cook, uncovered, stirring occasionally, until the peas are just tender, about 5 minutes. Taste and add more salt if needed.

Remove from the heat and stir in the cilantro and lemon juice. Serve at once.

Per serving: 200 calories, 8 g protein, 9 g fat (8 g sat), 24 g carbohydrates, 300 mg sodium, 49 mg calcium, 7 g fiber

There's something quite miraculous about wild mushrooms. They bring to the table what the French call *terroir*—the taste of place, of the earth—something cultivated mushrooms can only dream of.

WILD MUSHROOM ragoût

MAKES 4 SERVINGS

3 tablespoons extra-virgin olive oil

½ cup finely diced shallots

2 pounds mixed wild mushrooms (see tip)

2 tablespoons porcini mushroom powder (optional)

1 unsalted vegetable bouillon cube

½ teaspoon sea salt

½ teaspoon freshly ground black pepper

½ cup dry Marsala wine or dry sherry

2 tablespoons freshly squeezed lemon juice

2 tablespoons chopped fresh parsley or snipped chives

Heat the oil in a large saucepan over medium-high heat until fragrant, about 30 seconds. Add the shallots and cook, stirring frequently, until softened and lightly colored, 4 to 5 minutes. Don't let them brown. Add the mushrooms and stir well. Cover and cook until the mushrooms begin to release their liquid, 1 to 2 minutes. Add the optional porcini mushroom powder, the bouillon cube, salt, and pepper and stir well. Cook, stirring frequently, until the liquid is absorbed and the mushrooms begin to brown, about 5 minutes. Add the wine, stirring to incorporate any browned bits stuck to the pan into the sauce. Remove from the heat and add the lemon juice and parsley, shaking the saucepan back and forth to mix well. Serve at once.

Per serving: 193 calories, 11 g protein, 12 g fat (2 g sat), 14 g carbohydrates, 374 mg sodium, 17 mg calcium, 3 g fiber

TIP▶ Wild mushrooms can be difficult to find at certain times of the year, and they can be quite expensive. To work around these challenges, you can use a combination of button, cremini, and portobello mushrooms, along with whatever wild mushrooms you wish, such as chanterelle, porcini, or morel. You can also use dried wild mushrooms, but they must be reconstituted in water first and then drained and rinsed to remove any grit. If you choose this option, pour the soaking liquid through a towel to strain it, and then add it to the sauce for additional flavor.

Pattypan squashes, with their little hats just ready to detach, are obvious candidates for stuffing. This preparation is reminiscent of Italian stuffed squashes—creamy, slightly cheesy, and succulent. In fact, it's surprising how easily an unsuspecting person might mistake them for a dairy-rich version. I served these as an appetizer and invited an Italian friend for dinner. After digging into the first of three on her plate, she looked up and said, "Is this . . . vegan?" That kind of reaction is music to any cook's ears.

stuffed PATTYPAN SQUASH

MAKES 4 SERVINGS

8 pattypan squashes

1 tablespoon sea salt (optional)

2 tablespoons extra-virgin olive oil

½ cup finely diced shallots

4 cloves garlic, minced or pressed

Pinch sea salt

6 tablespoons Cashew Cream (page 19)

1½ tablespoons chopped fresh basil

1½ tablespoons mellow white miso

¼ teaspoon freshly ground black pepper

Cut the top third off the squashes to make little "hats." Using a small spoon, carve out the soft flesh from the center of the squashes, forming little cups. Set the cups and tops aside and coarsely chop the removed flesh.

Fill a large saucepan with water. Add the optional tablespoon of salt and bring to a boil over high heat. Add the squash cups and tops and cook until just tender, about 5 minutes. Drain and refresh the squashes under cold water. Drain on towels.

Heat the oil in a large saucepan over medium-high heat until fragrant, about 30 seconds. Add the shallots and cook, stirring frequently, until softened, about 3 minutes. Don't let them brown. Add the garlic, chopped squash flesh, and a pinch of salt and stir well. Cook, stirring frequently, until the squash is very tender, about 5 minutes. Remove from the heat and let cool slightly. Stir in the Cashew Cream, basil, miso, and pepper. Fill the squash cups with the mixture and top with the lids.

Put the filled squashes in a saucepan large enough to hold them all in a single layer and sprinkle 2 tablespoons of water around them. Cover and warm over medium heat until the squashes are heated through, about 4 minutes. Serve at once.

Per serving: 180 calories, 3 g protein, 12 g fat (1 g sat), 16 g carbohydrates, 314 mg sodium, 73 mg calcium, 4 g fiber

GRILLED
baby eggplants
WITH RAS EL HANOUT

Eggplants were made to be grilled. Their flavor deepens and grows exponentially when exposed to a hot iron, whether a skillet or a grill. They become luscious and sensual, with a smoky note behind every bite.

6 baby eggplants

1½ tablespoons ras el hanout or curry powder

½ teaspoon sea salt

2 tablespoons extra-virgin olive oil

1 tablespoon chopped fresh mint, cilantro, or parsley

Preheat an outdoor, electric, or stove-top grill on high heat.

Cut the eggplants in half lengthwise, including the stems. Cut a crisscross pattern deeply into the flesh of each half, taking care not to pierce the skins. Put the ras el hanout and salt in a small bowl and mix well. Rub the mixture into the cuts in the eggplants. Brush the cut sides of the eggplants with the oil and put them cut-side down on the grill. Cook for 2 to 3 minutes, depending on thickness. Turn over and cook until the eggplants are tender, 2 to 3 minutes. Serve at once, garnished with the mint.

Per serving: 148 calories, 0 g protein, 8 g fat (1 g sat), 13 g carbohydrates, 281 mg sodium, 10 mg calcium, 13 g fiber

If I had to list just ten comfort foods, ratatouille would be among the top five. For a cook, the smells associated with each step are sheer pleasure. The secret to a great ratatouille is twofold. First, sauté each vegetable separately, searing it and concentrating its essence before combining it with the other vegetables. Second, use fresh thyme rather than dried. It's really that easy. It also helps to cook the mixture very

ratatouille

MAKES 8 SERVINGS

4 Japanese eggplants (see tip)

4 medium zucchini

2 red bell peppers

2 green bell peppers

2 medium yellow onions

½ cup extra-virgin olive oil, plus more as needed

½ teaspoon sea salt, plus more as needed

½ teaspoon freshly ground black pepper

12 cloves garlic, thinly sliced

3 cups no-salt-added tomato purée

1 small bundle thyme sprigs, tied with kitchen twine

4 bay leaves

½ teaspoon Aleppo pepper (optional)

1 tablespoon red wine vinegar

2 tablespoons chopped fresh parsley

Cut the eggplants and zucchini crosswise into cylinders about 1½ inches thick. Cut the peppers and onions into 1½-inch squares. Keep each vegetable separate.

Heat 2 tablespoons of the oil in a large skillet over high heat until fragrant, about 30 seconds, swirling to spread the oil evenly. Put the eggplant in the skillet with one of the cut ends of each cylinder touching the skillet. Cook until lightly browned on the bottom, about 4 minutes. Turn each cylinder over and brown the other end, adding a little more oil, 1 tablespoon at a time, if needed. When both ends of the cylinders have been browned, shake the pan to topple the pieces and lightly sear the sides. Transfer the eggplant to a large bowl. Cook the zucchini in the same fashion. Add the zucchini to the bowl with the eggplant.

slowly, as this allows the flavors to intensify. The eggplant becomes unctuous and succulent, perfectly balanced by the mild acidity of the tomato, and the garlic mellows to a sweet background note. Serve this with rice, or in a bowl by itself, accompanied by thick slices of grilled bread.

Put 1 tablespoon of the oil in the skillet and then add the peppers. Sprinkle with some of the salt and black pepper. Shake the pan and stir to coat all the pieces with the oil. Cook the peppers, stirring frequently, until their skins begin to char, 5 to 7 minutes. Add the peppers to the bowl with the eggplant and zucchini.

Put 2 tablespoons of the oil in the pan and then add the onions. Sprinkle with some of the salt and black pepper. Cook, stirring frequently, until the onions are lightly browned, about 5 minutes. Add them to the bowl of vegetables.

Heat the remaining oil in a large saucepan over medium-high heat until fragrant, about 30 seconds, swirling to spread the oil evenly. Add the garlic and stir until it begins to brown and stick, 2 to 3 minutes. Add the tomato purée, the remaining salt and black pepper, and the thyme, bay leaves, and Aleppo pepper. Continue stirring until the mixture begins to bubble, 3 to 5 minutes. Add the eggplant, zucchini, bell peppers, and onions and stir well. Bring to a boil. Stir in the vinegar. Decrease the heat to medium-low, cover, and cook, stirring occasionally, until all the vegetables are very tender, about 2 hours.

Remove and discard the thyme bundle and bay leaves. Serve in shallow soup bowls, garnished with the parsley.

Per serving: 230 calories, 6 g protein, 11 g fat (1 g sat), 39 g carbohydrates, 189 mg sodium, 125 mg calcium, 11 g fiber

TIP▶ Japanese eggplants are long, thin eggplants, 1½ to 2 inches in diameter. This makes them perfect partners with zucchini, especially the way they are prepared in this dish.

RATAZITI▶ Toss leftover Ratatouille with cooked brown rice ziti. Of course, you could also combine it with any pasta shape you wish, but then you'd have to call it something else.

mustard greens
WITH DAIKON AND GOLDEN BEETS

MAKES 4 SERVINGS

Mustard greens can easily be overcooked. Very fresh young mustard greens can be cooked fairly briefly, retaining just enough crispness to be chewable. I much prefer them this way, both for health and pleasure.

2 large golden beets, scrubbed and cut into ½-inch dice

1 large daikon radish, scrubbed and cut into ½-inch dice

2 tablespoons extra-virgin coconut oil

14 very fresh young mustard greens, center ribs removed, coarsely chopped

¼ teaspoon sea salt

¼ cup mirin

2 teaspoons sriracha sauce

Steam the beets and daikon radish until just tender, about 15 minutes.

Heat the oil in a large saucepan over high heat until fragrant, about 30 seconds, swirling to spread the oil evenly. Add the mustard greens and cook, stirring briskly, until wilted, about 1 minute. Add the salt, mirin, and sriracha sauce and cook, stirring, constantly, for 1 minute. Add the beets and daikon radish and cook, stirring constantly, until the mustard greens are barely tender, 2 minutes. Serve at once.

Per serving: 169 calories, 2 g protein, 9 g fat (7 g sat), 19 g carbohydrates, 426 mg sodium, 43 mg calcium, 3 g fiber

Pears in Pomegranate Juice, page 134

Chocolate-Raspberry Tart, page 138

Romesco sauce is unsurpassed as an accompaniment to grilled foods, and among the best grilled candidates are asparagus and leeks. Choose the thickest asparagus and thinnest leeks you can find for the best results. This dish can be served on a plate with a grain or with white beans or other vegetables, but it's absolutely spectacular on its own as a first course.

grilled asparagus and leeks
WITH ROMESCO SAUCE

MAKES 4 SERVINGS

2 pounds asparagus

4 leeks

3 tablespoons extra-virgin olive oil

½ teaspoon sea salt

¼ teaspoon freshly ground black pepper

2 cups Romesco Sauce (page 30)

1 tablespoon chopped fresh parsley

Preheat an outdoor, electric, or stove-top grill on high heat.

Wash the asparagus well and snap off the tough ends. Arrange them in a single layer on a baking sheet. Cut the leeks in half lengthwise, including the roots and green parts. Wash under cold running water, spreading the leaves to rinse away any clinging dirt, and shake off the excess water. Lay on the baking sheet, cut-side up.

Brush the asparagus and leeks with the oil and sprinkle with the salt and pepper. Put the leeks on the grill, cut-side down, followed by the asparagus. Cook for 3 minutes, turn them over, and cook for 2 minutes longer. The vegetables should have light grill marks but still be a bit crunchy. Return them to the baking sheet. Cover with aluminum foil until ready to serve.

Divide the asparagus and leeks among four plates, arranging the vegetables parallel. Spoon about ¼ cup of the sauce across the vegetables, garnish with the parsley, and serve at once. Pass the remaining sauce at the table.

Per serving: 588 calories, 12 g protein, 51 g fat (6 g sat), 34 g carbohydrates, 542 mg sodium, 122 mg calcium, 12 g fiber

zucchini and corn WITH BASIL

In the summer, when the garden is ceaselessly pumping out young zucchini, it can be hard to keep up with them. If you have access to any zucchini blossoms, definitely include them in this dish. They add incredible depth of flavor.

8 very young zucchini, or 4 medium zucchini

3 tablespoons extra-virgin olive oil

1 large white or yellow onion, diced

4 cloves garlic, minced

2 ears white corn

½ teaspoon sea salt

¼ teaspoon freshly ground black pepper

8 zucchini blossoms, coarsely chopped (optional)

½ cup chopped fresh basil, lightly packed

Cut the young zucchini into ¼-inch rounds. If using medium zucchini, quarter it lengthwise first, and then cut it crosswise into ¼-inch slices.

Heat the oil in a large saucepan over high heat until fragrant, about 30 seconds, swirling to spread the oil evenly. Add the onion and garlic, and cook, stirring frequently, until soft, about 2 minutes. Add the zucchini and stir well. Cut the corn kernels off the cobs directly into the pot. Scrape the remaining starch off the cobs with the back of the knife into the pot. Stir well. Add the salt and pepper. Cook, stirring frequently, until the vegetables are tender, about 5 minutes. During the last minute of cooking, add the zucchini blossoms, if using, and stir well. Remove from the heat. Add the basil and stir well. Serve at once.

Per serving: 203 calories, 5 g protein, 11 g fat (2 g sat), 25 g carbohydrates, 303 mg sodium, 97 mg calcium, 5 g fiber

I've lost count of the times avowed spinach haters commented that after eating this dish they would have to reassess their stance on spinach. As it is with most problem foods, the problem turned out to be the way it had been prepared, not the spinach. Briefly blanching it removes most of the tannin, which I think is what makes eating it so objectionable. Tannin is what gives spinach that icky metallic taste and makes your teeth feel weird. With that out of the way, it's smooth sailing.

sautéed spinach
WITH ROASTED GARLIC AND ALEPPO PEPPER

MAKES 4 SERVINGS

2 pounds baby spinach

8 cloves Roasted Garlic (page 12)

3 tablespoons extra-virgin olive oil

2 teaspoons Aleppo pepper, or ¼ teaspoon cayenne

¼ teaspoon sea salt

¼ teaspoon freshly ground black pepper

Fill a large saucepan with water and bring to a boil over high heat. Add the spinach and stir once, making sure all the leaves are submerged. Immediately drain the spinach in a colander and refresh under cold running water. Squeeze as much water out of the spinach as possible. Put the spinach on a plate next to the stove.

Chop the garlic into small pieces, and then mash it into a paste using the flat side of the knife.

Heat the oil in a large skillet over medium-high heat until fragrant, about 30 seconds, swirling to spread the oil evenly. Add the garlic paste, Aleppo pepper, salt, and pepper and stir briskly until thoroughly mixed. Add the spinach and stir, tossing to combine it with the garlic mixture. Cook, stirring constantly, just until the spinach is warmed through. Serve at once.

Per serving: 157 calories, 6 g protein, 10 g fat (1 g sat), 8 g carbohydrates, 322 mg sodium, 329 mg calcium, 7 g fiber

Although this recipe looks long and complicated, just give yourself a little time, follow the instructions, and you'll see it's really no big deal. And at the end, you'll have a major showstopper to serve your guests. Go for it!

Mediterranean
EGGPLANT STACK

See photo facing page 87.

MAKES 4 SERVINGS

GARBANZO PURÉE

1 can (25 ounces) no-salt-added garbanzo beans, drained and rinsed

3 tablespoons mashed Roasted Garlic (page 12)

3 tablespoons extra-virgin olive oil

2 tablespoons freshly squeezed lemon juice

½ teaspoon ras el hanout

½ teaspoon sea salt

¼ teaspoon hot red chile powder or cayenne

SAUTÉED SPINACH

8 ounces baby spinach

1 tablespoon extra-virgin olive oil

2 cloves garlic, very thinly sliced

⅛ teaspoon sea salt

⅛ teaspoon freshly ground black pepper

Preheat the oven to 200 degrees F.

To make the garbanzo purée, combine the beans, roasted garlic, oil, lemon juice, ras el hanout, salt, and red chile powder in a food processor. Process until smooth. Scrape into an ovenproof bowl, cover tightly with foil, and put in the oven to warm.

To make the sautéed spinach, fill a large saucepan with water and bring to a boil over high heat. Add the spinach and stir for 1 minute. Drain in a colander and refresh under cold running water. Squeeze gently to remove as much water as possible. Heat the oil in a medium skillet over medium-high heat until fragrant, about 30 seconds, swirling to spread the oil evenly. Add the garlic, salt, and pepper. Cook, stirring constantly with a silicone spatula or wooden spoon, until the garlic turns light tan, 2 to 3 minutes. Immediately add the spinach and stir to thoroughly coat with the oil and garlic. Set aside.

STEWED ONION AND ROASTED PEPPERS

2 tablespoons extra-virgin olive oil

1 red onion, quartered and sliced ¼ inch thick

¼ teaspoon sea salt

⅛ teaspoon freshly ground black pepper

2 Roasted Red Peppers (page 14), quartered and cut into ¼-inch-thick slices

⅛ teaspoon smoked paprika

ARTICHOKES WITH CASHEW CREAM

1 can (14 ounces) water-packed artichoke hearts, drained and rinsed

1 tablespoon extra-virgin olive oil

2 teaspoons mashed Roasted Garlic (page 12)

1 teaspoon grated lemon zest

2 teaspoons freshly squeezed lemon juice

⅛ teaspoon sea salt

⅛ teaspoon freshly ground black pepper

¼ cup Cashew Cream (page 19)

To make the stewed onion and roasted peppers, heat the oil in a medium skillet over high heat until fragrant, about 30 seconds, swirling to spread the oil evenly. Add the onion, salt, and pepper and stir well to combine. Decrease the heat to medium, and cook, stirringly occasionally, until the onion begins to soften, 3 to 4 minutes. Add the peppers and paprika and mix well. Decrease the heat to medium-low, cover, and cook for 10 to 15 minutes, until the onion is very soft, stirring frequently to prevent the vegetables from sticking. Remove from the heat and keep covered.

To make the artichokes with cashew cream, put the artichoke hearts, oil, roasted garlic, lemon zest, lemon juice, salt, and pepper in a food processor. Pulse until coarsely chopped. Add the cashew cream and pulse until just combined. Scrape into an oven-proof bowl, cover tightly with foil, and put in the oven to warm. *(continued)*

GRILLED EGGPLANT

2 large eggplants, cut into
½-inch-thick slices

¼ cup extra-virgin olive oil

½ teaspoon sea salt

GARNISHES

1 Roasted Red Peppers (page 14), cut
into ¼-inch dice

4 tablespoons Roasted Garlic Purée
(page 12)

1½ tablespoons chopped fresh parsley

½ teaspoon freshly ground black
pepper

1½ tablespoons extra-virgin olive oil

To make the grilled eggplant, preheat an electric or stove-top grill on high heat. Brush the eggplant slices with the oil and sprinkle lightly with the salt. Working in batches if necessary, put the eggplant on the grill and cook until tender, 3 to 4 minutes per side. Transfer to a baking sheet and put in the oven to keep warm. When all the eggplant slices are done, begin assembling the stacks.

To assemble, put 4 of the eggplant slices in a single layer on a baking sheet. Put 2 to 3 tablespoons of the garbanzo purée in the center of each eggplant slice and spread with the back of a spoon to the edge. Layer with another eggplant slice on top of the purée and divide the spinach mixture equally among the stacks, spreading it evenly. Layer another eggplant slice on top of the spinach, and divide the roasted red pepper mixture equally among the stacks, spreading it to the edge of the eggplant slices. Top with the remaining eggplant slices and spread the artichoke mixture on top. Increase the oven temperature to 325 degrees F. Bake the eggplant stacks for about 10 minutes, until heated through.

To garnish and serve, put each eggplant stack in the middle of a dinner plate. Strew the roasted peppers around each stack. Add a few dabs of the garlic purée around the plate in a random pattern. Sprinkle the parsley all around. Finish with a sprinkling of the pepper and a drizzle of the oil. Serve at once.

Per serving: 607 calories, 16 g protein, 40 g fat (6 g sat), 58 g carbohydrates, 1,347 mg sodium, 263 mg calcium, 20 g fiber

Let's get something straight. Dessert was never meant to be food for the body. It's upliftment for the spirit. We don't eat it for our health; we eat it for fun. This leads to two important conclusions.

First, it's not a good idea to think of dessert as a regular part of a meal, something expected, as in "what's for dessert?" It's much wiser to think of it as an extraordinary treat for special occasions.

desserts

Second, as I'm fond of saying, if you're going to eat something that isn't terribly good for you, at least make sure it's terribly good. You're indulging yourself, and you deserve it, so make it count!

I've carefully designed the desserts in this chapter to provide maximum pleasure with the least possible compromise. I've included some elements that are actually quite healthful.

The purpose of life is joy. We were born for this. So when eating dessert, forget all notions of sin and decadence, pull out all the stops, and surrender to the divine pleasure of it.

This is a a bit like a deconstructed piña colada. I've separated the pineapple from the coconut and given it a delectable little char on the grill before adding it back in chunks. This treatment brings out the best in both of these tropical gems. *Piña quemada* literally means "burnt pineapple,"

piña quemada ICE CREAM

MAKES 4 CUPS

1 tablespoon maple syrup

1 tablespoon extra-virgin olive oil

3 slices fresh pineapple, each about ½ inch thick, skin and "eyes" removed

3 cups almond milk

4 teaspoons arrowroot, kuzu, or cornstarch

½ cup evaporated cane juice crystals

3 cups unsweetened shredded dried coconut

1 can (14.5 ounces) full-fat coconut milk

Pinch sea salt

Preheat an outdoor, electric, or stove-top grill on high heat.

Put the maple syrup and oil in a small bowl or measuring cup and stir until well combined. Brush the pineapple with the mixture and grill until marked, about 2 minutes. Turn over and grill the other side until marked, about 2 minutes. Transfer to a plate and let cool. Cut out the tough core portion in each pineapple slice, and then cut the slices into ½-inch cubes. Set aside.

Put ¼ cup of the almond milk and the arrowroot in a small bowl. Stir well and set aside.

Put the remaining almond milk and the evaporated cane juice crystals in a medium saucepan, stirring until the crystals are dissolved. Bring to a boil over medium-high heat. Stir in the coconut and return to a boil. Immediately remove from the heat,

but in this sense it means charred from the grill. *Colada* means "strained," but since the pineapple is being left in chunks instead of being blended, there's no need to strain out the fibers to obtain a smooth texture. This is a labor of love, so don't skimp on the attention required.

cover, and let cool. Strain into a bowl, pressing down firmly on the coconut to squeeze out as much liquid as possible. Pour the almond milk into a clean saucepan. Add the coconut milk and salt and bring to a simmer over medium heat. Stir the reserved arrowroot mixture well, and then whisk it into the hot coconut milk mixture. Continue whisking until the mixture thickens slightly, about 30 seconds. Remove from the heat and let cool, stirring occasionally to prevent a skin from forming on the surface. Refrigerate until cold, 4 to 6 hours.

Pour the mixture into an ice-cream maker and freeze according to the manufacturer's instructions. When the ice cream is nearly frozen but still pliable, fold in the pineapple, distributing it evenly. Scrape the ice cream into a chilled container and serve at once or freeze until firm.

Per ½ cup: 194 calories, 1 g protein, 12 g fat (8 g sat), 23 g carbohydrates, 76 mg sodium, 125 mg calcium, 1 g fiber

absinthe ICE CREAM

Absinthe, a spirit flavored with green anise, sweet fennel, and wormwood, is a delectable blend of sweet and bitter. I borrowed the idea of using absinthe and chocolate truffle bits as an ice-cream flavor from David Lebowitz, a gifted pastry chef. My version, of course, is nondairy. I've used pistachios because of their color (absinthe is also known as "the green fairy"), and because their flavor blends beautifully with the spirit's aromatics.

2 cups raw cashews, soaked in 2 cups water for 8 to 12 hours

1 cup water

1 cup shelled raw pistachios, soaked in hot water to cover for 2 hours

1 cup almond milk

1¼ cups evaporated cane juice crystals

6 tablespoons absinthe (see tip)

Pinch salt

1½ cups coarsely chopped Chocolate Ganache (page 20) or dark chocolate

Drain and rinse the cashews and put them in a blender with the water. Process on high speed until smooth. (A high-speed blender, such as a Vitamix, is ideal for obtaining the smoothest results.) Scrape into a bowl and rinse out the blender.

Drain the pistashios. Remove any skins and discard any of nuts that are dark, discolored, or showing signs of decay. This is somewhat painstaking, but it will produce a far superior result. Rinse the pistachios and put them in the blender. Add the almond milk and process until very smooth. Add the blended cashews, evaporated cane juice crystals, absinthe, and salt. Process until well blended. Pour into a bowl, scraping as much from the sides of the blender as possible. Cover the bowl tightly and refrigerate until cold, 4 to 6 hours.

Pour the mixture into an ice-cream maker and freeze according to the manufacturer's instructions. When the ice cream is nearly frozen but still pliable, fold in the ganache, distributing the pieces evenly. Scrape the ice cream into a chilled container and serve at once or freeze until firm.

Per ½ cup: 408 calories, 7 g protein, 19 g fat (5 g sat), 44 g carbohydrates, 21 mg sodium, 74 mg calcium, 4 g fiber

TIP▶ Absinthe doesn't appeal to everyone. If you're not fond of it, or if you're not sure and don't want to buy a bottle to find out, please don't let that deter you. This wonderful ice cream will be almost as good with a number of other pistachio-friendly options, such as Grand Marnier, white rum, curaçao, Cointreau, and even amaretto, to name a few. If you opt to omit the alcohol entirely, simply add 1 teaspoon of vanilla extract and ¼ teaspoon of almond extract. Of course, I highly recommend pistachio extract instead of the almond extract, but pistachio extract is quite difficult to find.

peach ice cream
WITH AMARETTO

Just a splash of amaretto adds a layer of bittersweet flavor to this already luscious dessert. Two tablespoons equals one ounce, which is the amount in a miniature bottle of liqueur, so don't feel like you need to buy a large bottle of amaretto just to make this one recipe. On the other hand, a bottle of amaretto doesn't seem to last very long in my house, so this may not be a problem for you.

1 cup plus 2 tablespoons water

½ cup plus 2 tablespoons evaporated cane juice crystals

2 cups diced ripe peaches, with skin

½ cup hempseeds

2 tablespoons amaretto (see tip)

2 teaspoons vanilla extract

Put ½ cup of the water and the evaporated cane juice crystals in a small saucepan over medium heat. Swirl constantly until the crystals have dissolved, about 20 seconds. Pour into a blender and add the remaining water, peaches, hempseeds, amaretto, and vanilla extract. Process until smooth. Pour into a bowl, cover, and refrigerate until cold, about 2 hours.

Pour the mixture into an ice-cream maker and freeze according to the manufacturer's instructions. Scrape the ice cream into a chilled container and serve at once or freeze until firm.

Per ½ cup: 167 calories, 4 g protein, 5 g fat (0.3 g sat), 28 g carbohydrates, 0 mg sodium, 24 mg calcium, 1 g fiber

TIP▶ If you'd rather not use alcohol, replace the amaretto with ½ teaspoon of bitter almond extract or regular almond extract.

When blood oranges are in season, it's time to celebrate them—juiced, of course, but also segmented and used in salads, salad dressings, sauces, cocktails, and (hello!) sorbet. Can you make this dessert with another kind of orange? Of course! Will it be equally amazing? Of course not! My view is, if you're going to eat something with this much sugar in it, for heaven's sake make it worthwhile.

BLOOD ORANGE sorbet

MAKES 4 CUPS

8 blood oranges

1 cup evaporated cane juice crystals, plus more as needed

1 cup filtered water

¼ cup freshly squeezed lemon juice, plus more as needed

Grate the zest from the oranges and set aside. Squeeze the juice into a bowl and remove any seeds. It's not necessary to strain the juice; a little texture is preferable.

Put the evaporated cane juice crystals and water in a small saucepan and bring to a boil over high heat. As soon as the mixture turns clear, remove from the heat and stir in the zest. Let cool completely, and then strain into a medium bowl. Add the blood orange juice and lemon juice and whisk until well combined. Taste and add more lemon juice or evaporated cane juice crystals if desired. Cover the bowl and refrigerate until cold, about 2 hours.

Pour the mixture into an ice-cream maker and freeze according to the manufacturer's instructions. Scrape the sorbet into a chilled container and serve at once or freeze until firm.

Per ½ cup: 162 calories, 1 g protein, 1 g fat (0 g sat), 40 g carbohydrates, 0 mg sodium, 41 mg calcium, 3 g fiber

Go for Extraordinary! Look for moro blood oranges, as they have the deepest red flesh and a more delicious taste and aroma than other kinds of blood oranges.

In Mexico, mangoes are almost always served with a squeeze of fresh lime juice, which makes them pop to life. In this sorbet, I've also added a generous splash of an orange muscat dessert wine from California called Essencia.

mango SORBET

MAKES 4 CUPS

¾ cup evaporated cane juice crystals, plus more as needed

¾ cup water

3 cups fresh mango cubes

½ cup freshly squeezed lime juice, plus more as needed

¼ cup Essencia orange muscat dessert wine or other dessert wine

Put the evaporated cane juice crystals and water in a small saucepan and bring to a boil over high heat. As soon as the mixture turns clear, remove from the heat. Let the syrup cool completely before proceeding.

Put the syrup, mango, lime juice, and wine in a blender and process until smooth. Taste and add more lime juice or evaporated cane juice crystals if desired. Pour into a bowl, cover tightly, and refrigerate until cold, about 2 hours.

Pour the mixture into an ice-cream maker and freeze according to the manufacturer's instructions. Scrape the sorbet into a chilled container and serve at once or freeze until firm.

Per ½ cup: 131 calories, 1 g protein, 0 g fat (0 g sat), 31 g carbohydrates, 0 mg sodium, 2 mg calcium, 2 g fiber

strawberries
WITH BALSAMIC VINEGAR

If you ever need a no-nonsense, very fast, unusual fruit dessert, this one is it. All you need is a few strawberries, a little red wine, a spoonful of powdered sugar, and a splash of aged balsamic vinegar. In Italian this dish is called *fragole al aceto* (strawberries with vinegar), but as with all things Italian, the recipe is both simpler than you think and not as simple as it sounds. The key is the balsamic vinegar, so make sure you use a high-quality one.

1½ pints ripe strawberries

3 cups red wine, preferably Pinot Noir

1 tablespoon powdered sugar

1½ tablespoons aged balsamic vinegar or
   Poor Man's Aged Balsamic Vinegar (page 10)

Wash the strawberries very quickly without hulling them and lay them on a towel to drain. Hull the strawberries with the point of a knife and put them in a bowl. Pour the wine over the strawberries and swirl the bowl just a bit to make sure they are all submerged. Let sit for 5 minutes. Drain, reserving the wine for another use (or just to enjoy as a beverage).

Put the strawberries in a clean bowl and sprinkle them with the sugar. Toss very gently with a silicone spatula. Drizzle the vinegar over them and toss once more. Divide among four dessert goblets or bowls. Drizzle any remaining vinegar over them and serve at once.

Per serving: 163 calories, 1 g protein, 0 g fat (0 g sat), 15 g carbohydrates, 8 mg sodium, 14 mg calcium, 2 g fiber

Back when I made this dessert for the first time, pomegranate juice was not yet widely available, so I had to juice the pomegranates myself. It was a true labor of love, involving twelve large pomegranates, a lot of pressing, and red-stained hands. These days, with bottled pomegranate juice easily accessible,

pears IN POMEGRANATE JUICE

See photo facing page 118.

MAKES 4 SERVINGS

4 ripe Bosc pears, with stems intact

4 cups pomegranate juice

7 green cardamom pods

1 bay leaf

Select a medium saucepan that will accommodate the pears snugly in an upright position, allowing space for the stems to fit with the lid in place.

Core the pears from the bottom to remove the seeds, leaving as much of the flesh as possible. Peel the pears, leaving the stems attached. Trim the bottoms slightly, so the pears can stand up straight. Put them in the saucepan and add the juice. It's normal for the pears to turn on their sides and float at first. If you have a large strainer, set it over the pears gently to keep them submerged.

Break open the cardamom pods and remove the seeds. Crush the seeds to a gritty powder in a mortar with a pestle or on a cutting board with the back of a wooden spoon. Add the cardamom seeds and bay leaf to the saucepan. Bring to a boil over high heat. Decrease the heat to medium and simmer until the pears are tender, 20 to 45 minutes. To test the pears for tenderness, insert a paring knife into the thickest part and lift. The pear should slip off easily. Using tongs, grasp the pears by the stems and lift them out of the saucepan, allowing several seconds for the juice to drain well. Set them on a plate.

Increase the heat to high and bring the juice to a boil. Boil until the juice is reduced to about ¾ cup, 5 to 7 minutes. It should be a fairly dense syrup, thick enough to coat a spoon. If any juice has accumulated around the pears, carefully tip the plate and let it run back into the saucepan. Remove from the heat and let the syrup cool for about 10 minutes. Discard the bay leaf.

it's quick work to get this project going. You can use any type of pear for this, but Bosc pears are best because they take longer to cook, which gives them more time to absorb the aromatic pomegranate juice, and they hold their shape well after poaching.

Using a large spoon, drizzle the syrup over the pears. Lift the pears with the tongs and transfer them to dessert plates. Drizzle again with the syrup and serve at once.

Per serving: 250 calories, 1 g protein, 0 g fat (0 g sat), 64 g carbohydrates, 0 mg sodium, 20 mg calcium, 6 g fiber

VARIATION▶ Chop 1 cup raw or roasted pistachios into ¼-inch-thick bits. Put the pistachios in a coarse strainer and shake to strain out any very fine, powdery bits. Put the chopped pieces in a medium bowl. After drizzling the pears with syrup, roll them in the pistachios until evenly coated. Carefully set the pears on dessert plates and pour a little of the syrup around them. Serve at once.

Hot desserts are always something special, and even though this one takes virtually no effort at all, it's a showstopper. Baking a dish *en papillote*, or in a parchment package, allows all the steam to remain contained, enriching the food and keeping it moist. The aroma that billows from the suddenly opened parchment packages will instantly conquer everyone within twenty feet. As sweet as this dish is, there is

bananas EN PAPILLOTE

1 tablespoon extra-virgin coconut oil

4 ripe bananas

6 tablespoons fruit-juice-sweetened apricot jam

2 vanilla beans

4 teaspoons dried lavender blossoms (optional)

Preheat the oven to 450 degrees F. Cut four square sheets of parchment paper, at least 14 inches wide. Fold them in half diagonally, unfold, and then rub the open side with the coconut oil.

Put a peeled banana on each sheet of parchment, with the curve next to the fold. Divide the apricot jam among the bananas, spooning small gobs down their length. Split the vanilla beans lengthwise and lay one half over each banana. Sprinkle the lavender blossoms over the bananas. Fold the parchment gently over the bananas, and starting at one corner, crimp and fold the paper, repeating all the way around the open side to form a seal. You should have four airtight semicircular packages. Put the packages on two baking sheets, without touching if possible. Bake for 9 minutes. Remove from the oven, slit the flat sides with a sharp knife, and gently slide

no added sugar in it beyond what the fruits themselves contribute. If you're entertaining, you can prepare the packages before dinner, and then excuse yourself briefly just after the meal to slip them into the oven. Nine minutes later, dessert is ready! Serve the bananas plain or accompanied by a scoop of Piña Quemada Ice Cream (page 126).

the bananas out onto four dessert plates, drizzling any accumulated juices on top. Serve at once.

Per serving: 190 calories, 1 g protein, 4 g fat (3 g sat), 39 g carbohydrates, 1 mg sodium, 6 mg calcium, 3 g fiber

Go for Extraordinary! Dried lavender blossoms were once difficult to find, but as their popularity has increased, they're now widely available. Be sure to buy them from a specialty store or natural food market to ensure that they are edible and have no chemical additives. If you're unable to find them, don't let that deter you from making this very simple dessert. I made it without the lavender blossoms for many years, and it was always well loved. Save the vanilla beans for another use; the seeds will remain intact for the most part and will infuse sauces and dressings very well.

CHOCOLATE-RASPBERRY **tart**

See photo facing page 119.

Chocolate and raspberries are a sublime combination. In this tart, raspberries are present as whole, fresh fruit; in spirit form, infusing the chocolate; and as a glaze in the topping. Your guests will assume you slaved for hours over this tart, but it's all accomplished in three very easy steps. On my birthday the first year I went vegan, people were wondering how I would manage my birthday cake without eggs, cream, or butter. I made this tart, and that put to rest the myth of vegans missing out on the good life.

ALMOND CRUST

1½ cups finely ground or chopped raw almonds

½ cup palm sugar

⅓ cup extra-virgin coconut oil

CHOCOLATE FILLING

4½ ounces dark chocolate, chopped

1 cup full-fat coconut milk

2 tablespoons framboise eau de vie or raspberry liqueur

TOPPING AND GLAZE

2 pints fresh raspberries

¾ cup fruit-juice-sweetened raspberry jam

See how to make a tart shell.
youtu.be/W8IiUgKMBMA

Preheat the oven to 350 degrees F.

To make the crust, combine the almonds, sugar, and oil in a medium bowl and work with your fingers to form a thick, crumbly paste. Press into an 8-inch fluted tart pan with a removable bottom. Use a one-cup measuring cup or similar small container to press and form an even inside edge. Refrigerate until firm, about 45 minutes.

Put the tart pan on a baking sheet and bake for 15 minutes. The crust will be puffy and slightly misshapen. Press the crust gently back into shape with the measuring cup. Return to the oven and bake for 7 minutes longer. Remove from the oven and set on a rack to cool completely before proceeding.

To make the chocolate filling, put the chocolate in a blender. Put the coconut milk in a small saucepan over medium heat. As soon as it begins to bubble around the edge, remove from the heat. Count 10 seconds and then pour over the chocolate in the blender. Add the liqueur and process until very smooth.

Pour half the chocolate mixture into the cooled crust. It should come about halfway up the inner side of the shell. Spread it out evenly, taking care not to get any on the rim.

Starting from the rim of the tart, arrange half the raspberries in tight concentric circles over the filling, pushing the berries down gently so they touch the bottom. End with one raspberry in the center. Pour the remaining chocolate mixture over them, filling in the spaces between the raspberry tops and covering them completely. Take care not to drip any filling on the rim. Layer the remaining raspberries on top of the chocolate, again in concentric circles, but don't press them down. Refrigerate the tart until the filling is firm, 2 to 4 hours.

To make the glaze, put the jam in a small saucepan and warm over medium-low heat, stirring constantly, until it melts. It should be fairly thick but runny enough to apply with a pastry brush. Pour through a strainer to remove any raspberry seeds, pressing down to extract as much liquid as possible. Using a pastry brush, very gently brush the melted jam over the raspberries, allowing a little of the excess to drip down between them and cover the filling underneath. When the entire surface of the raspberries is coated, set the tart aside for at least 10 minutes to let the glaze congeal.

To serve, hold the tart pan rim with one hand and push up gently on the bottom with the other hand to release the tart. Set the rim portion of the mold aside. Slip a knife very carefully between the tart shell and the bottom of the mold. Work the knife gently around until the tart comes away from the mold. Set the tart down on a cutting board and cut it with a hot, dry knife, bracing the rim with one finger on either side of the knife to keep the tart shell intact. Slide the knife under the cut portion and gently lift it out. Put the slice on a dessert plate. Repeat as needed. Serve at once.

Per serving: 420 calories, 7 g protein, 28 g fat (16 g sat), 36 g carbohydrates, 44 mg sodium, 74 mg calcium, 5 g fiber

There is no sexier fruit than a ripe fig. Maybe you'll want to disagree and bring up the mango, and you'd be making a good argument there. But, no, figs are it. There's a reason Italian men call a luscious woman a *figa*. Come to think of it, Mexican women sometimes call a handsome man *un mango*, so maybe it's a draw. But it's not a good

fresh fig tart
IN A PISTACHIO CRUST

PISTACHIO CRUST

1½ cups finely ground or chopped raw pistachios

½ cup palm sugar

⅓ cup extra-virgin coconut oil

CASHEW CREAM FILLING

2 cups raw cashews, soaked in 3 cups of water for 8 to 12 hours

¼ cup maple syrup

¼ cup water

3 tablespoons kirsch

TOPPING AND GLAZE

12 ripe figs

¾ cup fruit-juice-sweetened apricot jam

Preheat the oven to 350 degrees F.

To make the tart shell, combine the pistachios, sugar, and oil in a medium bowl and work with your fingers to form a thick, crumbly paste. Press into an 8-inch fluted tart pan with a removable bottom. Use a one-cup measuring cup or similar small container to press and form an even inside edge. Refrigerate until firm, about 45 minutes.

Put the tart pan on a baking sheet and bake for 15 minutes. The shell will be puffy and slightly deformed. Press it gently back into shape with the measuring cup. Return to the oven and bake for 7 minutes longer. Remove from the oven and set on a rack to cool completely before proceeding.

To make the cashew cream filling, drain and rinse the cashews, and then pat them dry with a clean towel. Transfer the cashews to a blender along with the maple syrup, water, and kirsch and process until very smooth. Scrape into a medium bowl, cover, and set aside. You can also prepare this step a day ahead and keep the cream refrigerated.

To assemble the tart, scoop the filling into the cooled tart shell and spread it out evenly, taking care not to get any on the rim.

idea to make a tart with ripe mangoes. I've done it, and they tend to drain juices faster than you can finish assembling the tart, and they slip all over when the tart is cut. Delicious, but a horrible mess. When you're done making this tart, you'll step back and feel great pride at the thing of beauty you've created.

Cut the stems off the figs but do not peel them. Quarter the figs lengthwise with a sharp knife. Starting with the outside edge, place the rounded bottoms of the figs against the rim of the tart shell. Once a ring of the figs is complete, begin another ring, placing each fig between the tips of two of the figs in the first ring, keeping them close enough to hide the filling. Repeat until the filling is covered and the figs create a decorative flower motif. For the center, cut a round piece from one of the figs and set it in the middle, covering the last of the fig tips.

To make the glaze, put the jam in a small saucepan. Warm over medium-low heat, stirring constantly, until it melts. It should be fairly thick but runny enough to apply with a pastry brush. Pour through a strainer to remove any pieces of apricot, pressing down to extract as much liquid as possible. Using a pastry brush, very gently brush the melted jam over the figs, allowing a little of the excess to drip down between them and cover the filling underneath. When the entire surface of the figs is coated, put the tart aside for at least 10 minutes to let the glaze congeal.

To serve, hold the tart pan rim with one hand and push up gently on the bottom with the other hand to release the tart. Set the rim portion of the mold aside. Slip a knife very carefully between the tart shell and the bottom of the mold. Work the knife gently around until the tart comes away from the mold. Put the tart down on a cutting board and cut it with a hot, dry knife, bracing the rim with one finger on either side of the knife to keep the tart shell intact. If the glaze has set sufficiently, it should keep the rest of the components in place, resulting in a gorgeous slice of tart. Slide the knife under the cut portion and gently lift it out. Repeat as needed. Serve at once.

Per serving: 505 calories, 10 g protein, 24 g fat (11 g sat), 59 g carbohydrates, 31 mg sodium, 80 mg calcium, 5 g fiber

warmed apricots
WITH CACAO NIBS AND APRICOT KERNELS

MAKES 4 SERVINGS

Ever hear of ambrosia? Supposedly, it's what the gods dine on atop Mt. Olympus. This is one possible version, with just a touch of slightly bitter crunch added to keep it terrestrial. Bear in mind that this is a seasonal dish and should only be attempted with ripe, succulent apricots. Like most fruit desserts, the fruit itself is nearly sufficient, and all the other players are there merely to provide a context, like adoring fans surrounding a rock star.

6 large ripe apricots

3 tablespoons palm sugar

3 tablespoons water

3 tablespoons amaretto

2 tablespoons cacao nibs

Cut the apricots in half lengthwise and remove the pits. Quarter them lengthwise and put them in a medium bowl.

Break the pits with a meat tenderizer or mallet and remove the kernels. Chop the kernels coarsely, into just 3 or 4 pieces each, and set them aside on a small plate.

Put the sugar and water in a small saucepan and bring to a boil over high heat, stirring until the sugar has dissolved and a syrup forms, about 30 seconds. Add the apricots and toss gently until coated and just warmed, about 1 minute. Remove from the heat and stir in the amaretto, apricot kernels, and cacao nibs. Divide among four dessert bowls or goblets and serve at once.

Per serving: 111 calories, 1 g protein, 3 g fat (2 g sat), 18 g carbohydrates, 14 mg sodium, 5 mg calcium, 4 g fiber

Go for Extraordinary! Crushed raw cacao beans are called "nibs," and they are an extremely healthful food with (reputedly) up to four times the antioxidant content of green tea. They're also a delicious, bittersweet, crunchy treat.

online shopping sources

AMAZON

amazon.com

Amazon offers an impressive array of culinary items, both equipment and ingredients.

THE SPICE HOUSE

thespicehouse.com

The Spice House is an excellent source for high-quality herbs and spices at very reasonable prices.

CHOCOSPHERE

chocosphere.com

At Chocosphere you can find high-quality chocolate and cocoa powder at competitive prices. I recommend the Callebaut extra-bittersweet bits (callets) 71% (10 kilo bag), and the Cacao Barry "Extra Brute" cocoa powder (1 kilo bag).

GOLD MINE NATURAL FOODS

goldminenaturalfoods.com

Gold Mine Natural Foods is a one-stop shopping source for macrobiotic ingredients, especially ones that may prove hard to find locally.

JB PRINCE

jbprince.com

JB Prince sells restaurant-quality kitchen tools and equipment at competitive prices.

NUTS.COM

http://nuts.com

Nuts.com offers great deals on organic nuts, seeds, dried fruit, cacao, flours, and more.

index

146

Book Publishing Co.

books that educate, inspire, and empower

To find your favorite vegetarian and soyfood products online, visit:
healthy-eating.com

Speed Vegan
Alan Roettinger
978-1-57067-244-6 • $19.95

Omega 3 Cuisine
Alan Roettinger,
Udo Erasmus, PhD
978-0-920470-81-7 • $19.95

Cookin' Crunk
Bianca Phillips
978-1-57067-268-2 • $19.95

Jazzy Vegetarian
Laura Theodore
978-1-57067-261-3 • $24.95

*Becoming Vegan:
Express Edition*
Brenda Davis, RD,
Vesanto Melina, MS, RD
978-1-57067-295-8 • $19.95

Artisan Vegan Cheese
Miyoko Schinner
978-1-57067-283-5 • $19.95

Purchase these health titles and cookbooks from your local bookstore or natural food store,
or you can buy them directly from:

Book Publishing Company • P.O. Box 99 • Summertown, TN 38483 • 800-695-2241

Please include $3.95 per book for shipping and handling.